SOUTH
africa

To Anne

from Geoff Show

& /HOT 2014

SOUTH africa

A WORLD CHALLENGED

Angus M. Gunn

LEGACY PRESS

Canadian Cataloguing in Publication Data

Gunn, Angus M., 1920-
  South Africa: a world challenged

  Includes index.
  Bibliography: p.
  ISBN 0-9692269-2-6

  1. South Africa—Politics and government—1978-   2. South Africa—Race relations. I. Title.
  DT779.952.G85 1989   968.06'3   C88-091286-3

First published 1987
Reprinted 1987
New expanded edition 1989

© 1987, 1989 Angus M. Gunn

Set by The Typeworks, Vancouver, in ITC Bookman, and printed by Hignell Printing Limited, Winnipeg, on #2 offset 60 lb.

Published by:
Legacy Press
Suite One
650 Clyde Avenue
West Vancouver, B.C.
V7T 1E2   CANADA

Cover design by David Coates.

To my wife, Ruth,
and to Heather and Angus, Jr.

Nor wild Romance nor Pride allured me here:
Duty and Destiny with equal voice
Constrained my steps: I had no other choice...
Something for Africa to do or say.

Pringle

Inscription on the Monument, Grahamstown,
commemorating the arrival of the first
British settlers in 1820.

Acknowledgements

I am greatly indebted to many people for their assistance in the preparation of this book. It is quite impossible to do justice to all of them. Some names, however, are imprinted on the memory and I list them here with sincere thanks for the help they have afforded me. To the many others who have helped, I add my apologies for my failure to mention them by name: John Earle, University of the Witwatersrand; Rick Elphick, Wesleyan University; Rodney Davenport, John Daniel and Robert Fincham, Rhodes University; Alan Webster, Natal Department of Education; Erich Leistner, Africa Institute; Mangosuthu Buthelezi, Chief Minister of KwaZulu and President of Inkatha; Bok Marais, Human Sciences Research Council; Friede Dowie, South African Federated Chamber of Industries; Pierre Rossouw, Dutch Reformed Church; James Clarke, Assistant Editor, The Johannesburg *Star*; last, but by no means least, Angus, Jr., who helped immeasurably in design, illustration, and manuscript preparation.

A.M.G.

One of the most intriguing features of international
politics in the years following World War Two has been
the emergence of the pariah state. Pariah states are
countries that have been subjected to varying degrees of
ostracism, ostensibly on humanitarian grounds....The
label is now applied solely to those pro-Western
countries that, for one reason or another, have incurred
special displeasure on the part of the Soviet bloc or the
Third World....Of all these nations, South Africa has
perhaps elicited the most dislike from the United
Nations, the powers of the Warsaw Pact, and those
Western liberals who always see the mote in the eye of
their ally and never the beam in the eye of their enemy.

L. H. Gann and Peter Duignan
South Africa: War, Revolution, or Peace

Contents

Facing up to power sharing, from the *Clarion Call*, a publication of the government of KwaZulu

Why This Book?

North Americans tend to prescribe cures for which there are no diseases.

Frederik van Zyl Slabbert

South Africa is a developed, modern country, but its unique mix of people makes it also a developing nation. It is a complex society, difficult to understand, with a history that is deeply intertwined with crises in the British Empire, France, Germany and Southern Africa. The country was born in, and has lived with turmoil. At the beginning, in the year 1652, when Jan van Riebeeck established a Dutch supply station at Cape Town, Britain declared war on Holland. It was an omen of the violence that would be unleashed in later centuries on the descendants of those first settlers.

In the years that followed the seventeenth-century settlement at the Cape, inequalities and envies fanned the flames of conflict. The Bantu tribes that migrated southward fought for land repeatedly, first with the native Hottentots, then with one another, then with the trekkers who were migrating northward. The struggle for survival gave rise to numerous encounters, including bloody inter-tribal fights. As outlined in chapter two, thousands of Black warriors were often killed in a single phase of warfare. Sometimes whole tribes were wiped out.

A worldwide criticism of South Africa has been a feature of Western press and television alike. At times these attacks have reached a feverish pitch and have been accompanied by acts of vandalism and protest, often by people who know very little about the country. These excesses might be less frequent if levels of understanding were higher. Indeed, ignorance of South Africa is sometimes so great that fantasy and mythology, rather than limited knowledge, become the bases for judgment. A balanced view of both historical and current trends is urgently needed. This book has been written to meet such a need. It deals with information factually rather than polemically. In particular, it avoids the most common weakness of Western media: the use of the opinions and observations of selected individuals as primary sources of information.

The forebears of the present government leaders, descendants of the original Dutch settlers plus Huguenots and others who arrived later, parted company with the colonial authorities at the Cape shortly after the English had taken over the settlement by force. About 150 years ago they migrated northward in what has come to be known as the Great Trek, contending along the way with unfriendly neighbors and unknown territory, using resources that were frequently inferior to those of the Blacks. Their homes were woven rushes on a light framework of poles with bare earth floors. Furniture was made of the same rough, unseasoned timber as was used in the main structure. Locks and windows were as rare as newspapers.[1] They were subjected to repeated conflicts with both Blacks and English Whites. The tightly-knit community, forged under these privations, developed a fierce loyalty to one another and a determination to retain all of the territory occupied along the way.

Thus, when their descendants, the Afrikaners, finally came to power in 1948, they were determined to establish a separate territory for themselves, based on White majority rule. They regarded the homelands of the Blacks as separate nations. Modifications to traditional apartheid laws were introduced. These changes severely limited the educational opportunities for Blacks and prevented them from gaining experience in skilled occupations. It was a short-sighted and unfair policy. The nation was rapidly forsaking its rural roots as it changed into an industrial society, and an educated and skilled Black workforce would soon be indispensable to economic growth.

Apartheid, the economic and social segregation of peoples of different cultures, is neither new nor restricted to South Africa. It is a common pattern in multi-ethnic countries throughout the world. In the early settlement at the Cape it became established practice within the first few years. Later,

laws were introduced to make territorial segregation a permanent feature of South African life.[2] The world community
paid little attention to these changes when they were introduced. The outcry came much later, when the new government took office, in 1948, and placed on the statute books a
large number of laws and regulations affecting urban
Blacks. What had formerly been a partly legal, partly informal pattern of segregation was now perceived as a new system of White control over Blacks, just when the colonial yoke
was being discarded all over the globe.

Paradoxically, it was a live-and-let-live attitude on the part
of the early Afrikaners that created a need for new apartheid
laws. Unlike that of settlers in Australia, Canada, and the
U.S., where the social and economic structures of the native
tribes were frequently destroyed by European immigrants,
the philosophy of the Afrikaner was to leave Blacks in their
traditional territory with the culture intact.

One of the common Western responses to apartheid is a
clamor for one-man-one-vote in a unitary state, despite the
fact that such a franchise is rare elsewhere in the world. In
Canada, a national government vote in one province can
sometimes be worth three or four in another.[3] Furthermore,
in divided societies such as those found in Africa, there is a
need for a different system of voting, one that promotes consensus rather than majority rule.[4]

People look for familiar parallels when faced with complexity; Europe sees the problems of South Africa as delayed
decolonization, while the U.S. perceives another civil rights
struggle. Both of these images are false. Afrikaners were permanent residents of South Africa when ninety percent of
North America was still in the hands of its native peoples.
Slavery never reached the North American levels of abuse,
and was abolished throughout South Africa a generation before the corresponding action in the U.S. If there is a South
African parallel to Blacks in the U.S., it is in the colored community, a group whose history and present situation are the
results of actions by Whites.

At the 1988 Moscow Summit, Mikhail Gorbachev quoted a
Russian proverb in his welcoming address to Ronald
Reagan: "Better to see once than hear a hundred times."
Many of South Africa's most vocal critics have urged West-
erners to heed this advice, to get involved in the problems of
the country, at least to the point of being willing to see condi-

South Africa today

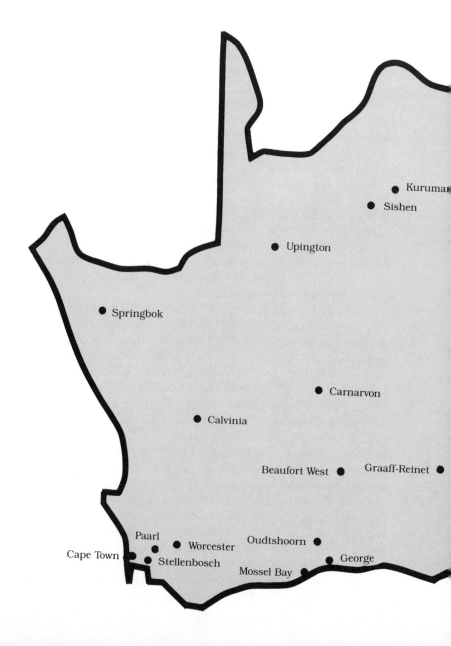

Kuruman

Sishen

Upington

Springbok

Carnarvon

Calvinia

Beaufort West

Graaff-Reinet

Paarl

Worcester

Oudtshoorn

Cape Town

Stellenbosch

George

Mossel Bay

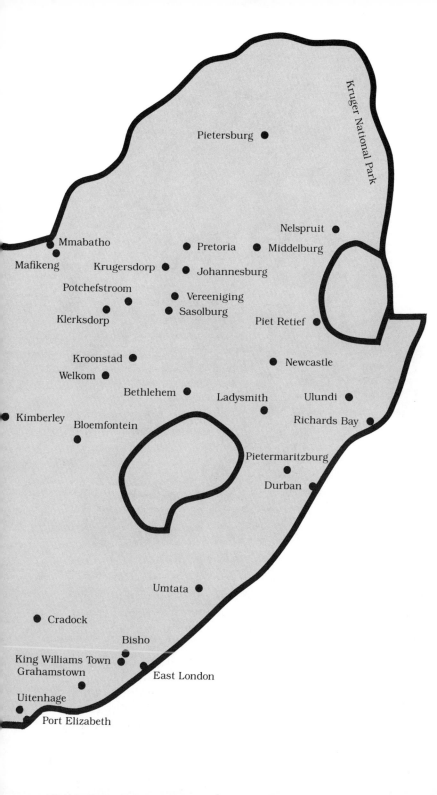

Cultural and sporting events are usually multi-racial

tions for themselves. Helen Suzman, a long-time liberal
critic of apartheid, maintains that investment, not divestment, is the answer to apartheid, because power comes out
of the end of a wallet.

The one-minute-to-midnight syndrome is yet another familiar fantasy. Every time violence flares up, in Soweto or
Durban, the doomsday writers predict the imminent fall of
the present government. This theme was familiar in 1962.
More than a quarter of a century later, headline-writers are
repeating the prediction. In fact, as is well-known to those

close to the situation, it is far too early to expect revolutionary changes. The minorities that are committed to violence still think they can win by force, in spite of the failure of their so-called peoples' revolution in 1986. In addition, recent surveys show that most South African Blacks are more interested in jobs and educational advancement than in political power.

Judging past events by present-day standards is a common mistake, but it is contrary to every known norm of history. The past must always be judged on its own terms. Notions of distinct races, with Whites having higher levels of intelligence than Blacks, was a widely-accepted view throughout Europe and North America in the last century. The scientific community provided what it thought was firm supporting evidence.[5] In the South African context, the existence of these views in old textbooks was a sample of the world's conventional wisdom, not evidence that the apartheid laws were rooted in nineteenth-century racial theories.

A parallel situation exists among those who left South Africa in the early 1960s, some because of past terrorist activities that now prevent them returning. These people see the country as it was when they left. They feel strongly, and rightly, about the injustices of that period, but unfortunately continue to campaign against conditions that no longer exist. They are the ones that prescribe cures for non-existent diseases. A typical demand from these people is the cry for desegregated sports, an aspect of South African life that has been free from a color bar for more than a decade.

South Africa: A World Challenged begins with a look back at the evolution of the nation. It is a story of many parts, a mosaic created by many peoples, each with its own distinctive culture. Part One is devoted to these historical threads. Some of the events seem far-removed from present day conditions, yet they still influence the political decisions of our times.

The contemporary scene is one of many crises, heightened by a worldwide pariah image. These crises include water shortages, especially in the urban areas, rapid population growth, social tensions, media distortions, political protests, and terrorist attacks from neighboring countries. Part Two deals with these challenges. Reporters frequently assume that their North American readers or viewers know much more about South Africa than they do. They use unusual terms and refer to little-known people. For these reasons a detailed glossary has been added to this new and expanded edition.

Exaggerated reports of the conflicts that erupt periodically in the urban townships tend to mask the gains that have been made both in resolving conflicts and in raising living standards. Even in the midst of violence, hundreds of thousands of workers from neighboring countries still choose to come to work in South Africa. The wages, health provisions, and overall lifestyle are seen to be better than the corresponding conditions in their own countries.

Part Three deals with the contexts within which many reforms are now taking place. To those South Africans who want to grab power by violent revolution, the reforms are too little, too late. To others, the pace of change is far too rapid. The government is faced with the gigantic task of charting a path of reform that will be acceptable to the majority. Many of the laws that are now undergoing change have been vehemently criticised for many years. Now that the process of change has begun, the inevitable tide of rising expectations tends to demand far more than is possible in a given time period.

Since 1977, there has been a growing recognition that the apartheid laws were a mistake, and their repeal urgent. Consequently, over the past ten years, despite widespread criticism that government actions have been purely cosmetic, there is an impressive record of apartheid-dismantling legislation:

1977 Racial restrictions on sports eliminated
1978 Ninety-nine year leases for Blacks in major urban
           areas
1979 Black trade unions recognized and given the right to
           strike
1980 Hotels, libraries, restaurants desegregated
1981 Blacks given permanent residence in "White" areas
           Compulsory school attendance for Blacks
1982 Local self-government for Blacks
           Blacks join government
1983 Coloreds and Indians elected to Parliament
           Job reservations scrapped
1984 New constitution abolishes Whites-only Parliament
           Political parties can recruit from any ethnic group

1985	Mixed Marriages Act scrapped
	Forced removals permanently stopped
	One citizenship for South Africans of all ethnic groups
1986	Pass laws and pass books abolished
	All-White provincial legislatures removed
	Homeland Blacks given South African citizenship
1987	Multi-ethnic new provincial executives
	Multi-ethnic regional services councils
	KwaZulu Natal Joint Executive: South Africa's first.
1988	Increased autonomy given to the self-governing states
	Multi-racial policy-making body for national affairs created
	Elected regional executives for Blacks outside homelands

North Americans have their greatest difficulties with South Africa when it comes to the rate of change. They find it very hard to remember that Africa, in this sense, is not New York. Sydney Maree, the famous international runner, who grew up in a Black township near Pretoria and understands the slow pace of change in a Black culture, hopes that the South African government will take plenty of time to raise standards of education among his fellow-citizens. "Only in that way", he says, "will Blacks be able to play a full role in the National Government."[6]

More than one hundred years ago Alexis de Tocqueville wrote: "The most perilous moment for a bad government is when it seeks to mend its ways. Only consummate statecraft can enable a king to save his throne when, after a long spell of oppressive rule, he sets to improving the lot of his subjects." In the history of apartheid, Blacks have experienced oppressive rule and they carry scars of resentment. Now, in light of de Tocqueville's words, the South African government faces the supreme task of undoing past errors and restoring trust.

Angus M. Gunn
West Vancouver, B.C.

Part One

The Historical Mosaic

In 1652, the year after Cromwell's Navigation Acts threw down the English challenge to the Dutch, Jan van Riebeeck landed in Table Bay with the first true European settlers ever to land on African soil south of the Sahara. What began as a cabbage patch on the way to India became one of the most vital strategic points in the entire Empire of the Dutch East India Company.

C. W. De Kiewiet
A History of South Africa

Earth as seen from the moon

1 | Global Village

*We have learned to be citizens of the world,
members of the human community.*

Franklin D. Roosevelt
Fourth Inaugural Address, 1945

For centuries, communities throughout the world lived independent lives, often self-sufficient, even when located at walking distances from one another. Villages in Iran, Mexico, and China were subsistence-style settlements of this kind. In the far north, beyond the Arctic Circle, native people built their homes of snow or rough frameworks covered with animal skins. Food was obtained by hunting or fishing. Clothing came from the furs of animals. There was little trade or human contact with the rest of the world. The changes from these age-old patterns of life came slowly. Rising standards of living coupled with the development of technology first led to travel beyond one's cultural hearth, then to exchanges of goods and ideas.

By the late 1960s, almost overnight it seemed, our planet's mosaic of settlements began to change rapidly. Ease of travel, worldwide television coverage, and, most of all, the advent of the battery-operated transistor radio, brought revolutionary changes in the ways people perceived one another. In the process, there emerged a homogeneity in lifestyles, an acceleration in exchanges of all kinds, and thus a newly-interdependent world of the kind envisaged by Marshall McLuhan when he coined the phrase 'global village'.

Space travel speeded up these developments. As astronauts soared outward toward the moon, they sent back pictures of an earth that looked very much smaller than anyone had ever realized. In fact it appeared no bigger than the spaceship itself. Comparisons soon followed. The spacecraft was a single, interdependent system. A breakdown in any one part could seriously endanger the lives of all who were aboard. Similarly, with the earth, toxic wastes or ozone-destroying chemicals discharged into the atmosphere by one nation could kill millions of people in all parts of the globe. With advancing technology, even one person could profoundly affect all of humanity. No country could any longer claim to be independent of the whole; nor could the whole feel that one part was dispensable due to its form of government or social structure. Our planet had become one single indivisible system. Peaceful coexistence was now a necessity.

Where there were similar values and lifestyles, the new interdependence was profitable; trade flourished, and standards of living rose. Where there was tension, as between the so-called first and third worlds, the new awareness of differences in wealth led to friction, then to alliances designed to correct the imbalances. The scale of correction needed, however, was far more easily defined than done. Many of the richer nations argued that it was impossible to redress huge differences in wealth simply by redistribution. Cartels were formed by nations owning the raw materials needed by the wealthier, industrialized nations, in order to push up prices. Unfortunately, the result was a slowing down of world economic activity and a lowering of demand for these raw materials.

Behind the safety of national boundaries the dialogue between the first and third worlds has continued, ostensibly seeking a solution to these disparities in wealth. There have been plans for a New Economic Order (NEO), mainly at the instigation of the United Nations, to try to shift the centres of economic power away from the richer nations. The net result of more than a decade of this effort must be regarded as negligible, because serious disparities in health, wealth, and social services still remain, and are likely to be greater than they are now when this century ends.

During the 1970s and 1980s, the volume of international exchanges of all kinds reached a new level. The micro-computer, sophisticated satellite communication systems, and new technologies which minimized the need for traditional raw materials, all contributed to this new phase of global village life. Information became the source of power so that, while dependence on other nations for the basic raw materials lessened, the race for the latest information accelerated.

In stock market transactions, for example, the mid-1980s saw an annual total of US$85 trillion in foreign exchanges, more than twenty times the value of all the world's international trade.[7]

In Japan the information revolution has reached new heights of quality and volume, seriously challenging the traditional leadership position of the U.S. There are many indicators of the primacy accorded information in this Asian nation. Literacy rates are the world's highest; the U.S., by contrast, is fifteenth.

Education has long been given top priority in Japan. Examinations begin at kindergarten level, and pressure for high performance increases in successive grade levels. By the time a student reaches the last two years of high school, evening classes for exam preparation take up as much time as day school. As a result, achievement levels are high: 10 percent of the nation's young people has an intelligence quotient over 130; the corresponding figure in North America is 2.

There is a massive support system for education. Book publishers release twice as many new titles annually per capita as do their North American counterparts. Furthermore, these new titles include many that have not been written by Japanese. Most of them, in fact, originate in Europe or the U.S. and are made available in both English and Japanese. Consequently, Japanese students have an intimate knowledge of other Western countries. Newspapers provide an impressive addition to this wealth of information, since the average per capita circulation exceeds that of almost all other nations.

The quality of the information available is as impressive as the quantity. There are more Japanese full-time correspondents in, for example, a major European country, than a typical North American weekly news magazine has in the entire world. The daily circulation figures for newspapers are enormous, reaching as high as 8 million, enabling management to maintain private fleets of aircraft. Facilities such as these bring quick and accurate reports of events in Japan, Korea, and the neighboring regions of the Soviet Union and China.

In the world of electronic media, the flow of information far exceeds that of print media. There are thousands of radio and television stations in Japan, most of which transmit educational programs only. Even where a station is classified as providing general interest programming, less than one third of the time is devoted to entertainment. The largest network in the country issues free television sets to most of the nation's classrooms, and supplements the gifts with textbooks that match the educational telecasts. Foreign observers have frequently rated the quality of Japanese television programs as better that those of North America in both depth of analysis and objectivity.

The economic implication of accurate and adequate information is evident worldwide. Manufacturing, a generation ago the main source of income, now accounts for only one fifth of all business returns. Half of the work force in a modern country is employed in communications. Rapid translation is an important part of such work. In one recent demonstration, an African, who spoke Swahili, communicated via satellite with a Canadian Inuit in the Far North; a reply was sent back in the Inuit language and, through a computer-translation program, was received almost instantly in Swahili.

Japanese firms, in close partnership with the nation's political leaders, are moving away from manufacturing into high-technology services such as the computer-translation system. North Americans are experiencing severe challenges from these developments. Even the long-standing traditions of Japanese public education are giving way to private methods which promote alternative ways of learning. Within the past few years, plans for sixteen new, corporately-sponsored universities have been approved by government. These institutions will stress science and technology with an emphasis on global systems.

Japan, therefore, is the outstanding example of a country which has harnessed the power of information to gain a leadership position in the application of technology. Furthermore, in this process, loyalty to the national interest draws government and business together in a high degree of cooperation. By contrast, North America has yet to realize the significance of the information revolution: our education, media, and economy still lag well behind their potential. Private enterprises focus their efforts in divergent, and at times international ways, to the detriment of the national interest. One example of this latter tendency is provided by the media. While governments make every effort to isolate

South Africa, the press and television maintain a disproportionate flow of information about that nation.

The major Western industrial nations are today using 40 percent less steel, and 30 percent less oil than they did in 1970. These reductions are due to design changes, such as new jet aircraft that cut fuel consumption by almost half, automobiles that run on 25 percent less gasoline, and microwave ovens that consume only 5 percent of the amount of electricity needed by a conventional oven. At the beginning of the 1970s, the prestigious Club of Rome forecast a severe shortage of raw materials by the mid-1980s; mining companies spent billions of dollars on new mines, in expectation of sharp increases in prices.[8] Their hopes never materialized, and their costly mistake was an illustration of the difficulty of long-term economic forecasting.

South Africa is probably the only country in the world where significant first and third world societies coexist within a single national territory. The country does not have the luxury of debating the differences from either side of an international border, as does the rest of the world. The problems of traditional disparities, in the context of the information revolution, have to be faced head-on until a solution is found. Paradoxically, in the face of intense international ostracism, South Africa's involvement in the world community is increasing.

Since the country is the Western world's principal supplier of gold, every market scare and every outburst of violence within South Africa sends gold prices soaring on the world's stock exchanges. Tourism, one of the fastest-growing industries anywhere, is drawn to countries that have the following six characteristics: (a) safety; (b) plenty to see and do; (c) scenic beauty; (d) friendly people; (e) reasonable cost-of-living; (f) unique lifestyles. South Africa fits these requirements perfectly; hence, there have been steady increases in tourist numbers—a 20 percent increase in 1987 over 1986 from Europe, and 46 percent from Japan.[9] Yet another of the nation's growing ties with the rest of the world is evident in a rapid growth of trade with the rest of the African continent.[10]

In 1988, 100 feature films were made in South Africa, more than in any other country. People from many nations have been watching and enjoying these films, as unaware of their origin as are North American drivers of sources for the chrome on their automobiles. A recent report from the U.S.

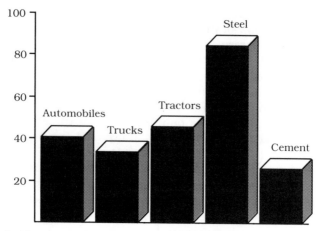

South Africa's production as percentages of the African total

Chamber of mines points out that a ban on such South African minerals as chrome, manganese, platinum, and, surprisingly, coal, would cost the United States US$4 billion annually, or US$19 billion over a four-year period.[11] In ways such as these, the country is a major player in an increasingly interdependent world.

One side effect of the information revolution is a shift from traditional ideological control of a nation's policies. Socialist administrations in several countries have become advocates of the free market, while conservatives have often shifted to a pragmatic blend of different ideologies. Even the Soviet Union has moved from its highly authoritarian stance to a more open society. All of this is highly relevant to South Africa, where the complexity of society has spawned a virtual torrent of theoretical constitutional and economic models. These range from a return to rigorous apartheid to decentralization into hundreds of tiny units, each of which chooses its own political and economic systems.

South Africa has an extraordinary variety of landscapes, languages and social conditions. There are villages where thousand-year-old tribal practices persist. There are cities where lifestyles correspond to those of urban centers anywhere in the Western world. There are dozens of languages so different from one another as to make communication a national problem. Even the natural environment is rare in its range of wildlife. Kruger National Park, with its more than four million acres of natural habitat, includes lions, elephants, giraffes, cheetahs, and hundreds of species of birds; it is a treasury of the wildlife of a continent.

Until the middle of the last century, South Africa was relatively poor, almost wholly dependent on a pastoral economy. Then came the discovery of diamonds followed by a series of additional discoveries of rich mineral deposits. In this century, the country has emerged as one of the world's richest mineral depositories. It supplies more than half of the Western world's demand for gold, manganese, vanadium, and is a major supplier of chrome, platinum, gem diamonds. Mineral wealth is the basis of the country's modern economy, one that is far ahead of any other in Africa.

The country's gross national product has doubled over the past decade, and still remains larger than that of any other African country of comparable population size. There are two additional indicators of this developed economy: levels of urbanization and health standards. In Africa as a whole 32 percent of the total population lives in urbanized areas. In South Africa the corresponding figure is 52. No other major African country south of the Sahara has so large a proportion of its people living in urban centres. Life expectancy and infant mortality rates are also better than in other parts of the continent: a life expectancy of 63 against a continental average of 53, and infant mortality at 78 as opposed to a continental average of 111 per thousand.[12]

South Africa's mining industry is the world's second biggest after the Soviet Union. It employs over 700,000 people, more than in Canada and the United States combined. Many of the miners are immigrants from neighboring countries. Blacks, the biggest group of workers, have seen their wages triple in real terms within the past decade. There are now more Black-owned cars in South Africa than there are private cars in all of the Soviet Union.

In spite of all its modernity, South Africa is still in many ways a typical African nation. Over the past three decades, mainly as a result of improved health services, the less developed countries of the world have experienced phenomenal growth in their total population. In recent years this rapid growth has slowed down to the point where the world's average is less than 2 percent annually. Africa, however, seems to have been the last to experience this drop. Its current average is 3 percent. South Africa is about 2.6, much higher than the world average, and very much higher than the developed world of North America, which has less than 1 percent, or Europe, with only 0.3 percent.

Social tensions are an additional source of difficulty. All over Africa the legacy of its colonial history is seen in the clash between tribal and national loyalties. Political boundaries were drawn with little regard to the traditional cultural patterns; thus, the Ovambo people are found today in Southern Angola and Northern Namibia, and the Tswanas are found in Botswana and South Africa. Much of the bloodshed from inter-tribal conflicts, both in South Africa and throughout the continent, is a direct result of the lines drawn on maps by the ruling European powers.

The high rates of population growth are pushing people off the land and into the cities, resulting in traditional rural societies being broken up and replaced by burgeoning shantytowns. Age-old norms of authority disappear in these communities and rivalry between different tribal groups leads to violence and crime. Governments soon discover that if they do not take firm measures, control of local gangs is lost. The new settlements can easily become ungovernable. South Africa's urban influx controls have prevented the emergence of the unhealthy ghettos found elsewhere in Africa.

African countries frequently discriminate against Westerners, Asians, religious groups, and tribes that happen to be out of favor. It would be hard indeed to find a genuine multi-racial society anywhere on the continent. Nevertheless, in spite of the absence of guiding models from other countries, South Africa is pressing ahead with plans to develop a truly democratic, multi-racial society.

Taken together, these two word pictures of South Africa—a highly developed modern economy, and a typical African society, with people concentrated in rural areas or suburban townships—reflect the human condition worldwide. They correspond to the terms we so frequently use to define the 'haves' and the 'have nots' of the world, that is first and third worlds.

The unique South African reality, already noted, is that these two worlds are placed together within the boundaries of a single country, not conveniently separated by political units. Quite apart from the economic disparities, there are the deeper cultural gaps which must be recognized. These are much more difficult to bridge. Experiences in Lebanon, Cyprus, and Ireland, show that power-sharing does not work as it might in North America when dealing with a multiracial society.

Most South Africans agonize over the problems of these two worlds. There is some progress. In the manufacturing sector as a whole, for example, from the early seventies to the early eighties, Black wages jumped 70 percent, in real terms, while those of Whites dropped by approximately 1 percent. The traditional differential is therefore decreasing, unlike most of the rest of the world where the rich continue to get richer and the poor poorer. Professor Paul Ehrlich is a well-known biologist and population dynamics expert from Stanford University, who has been making pessimistic predictions about the third world for the past 15 years. Recently he visited South Africa and came away with a very optimistic view of its future.[13]

South Africa thus becomes a microcosm of humanity, a mirror of the world. It is the place where the problems of relative wealth and poverty have to be tackled, and where the rights of minority groups have to be recognized. Perhaps these are some of the reasons for the worldwide preoccupation with this land at the southern tip of Africa. The intensity of our interest may also be due to more personal concerns; is this country an irritant, a challenge to our consciences, as we look at the disadvantaged within our own borders?

Students at Witwatersrand University protesting the government's emergency regulations

2 | Black Power

There must be, not a balance of power, but a community of power.

Woodrow Wilson
Address to the Senate, 1917

The story of South Africa begins with its original yellow-skinned inhabitants, the herders called Hottentots, who occupied the coastal areas in the south of the country, and the Bushmen who lived in the interior, subsisting by hunting and gathering. There are very few of these people left now, perhaps less than 50,000, due to the successive invasions by Blacks and Whites who drove them from their traditional habitats into the least hospitable regions of the country, on or near the Kalahari Desert.

These two native peoples of South Africa, collectively known as Khoisan, were nomads. The Hottentots were always on the move in search of new pastures for their sheep and cattle; the Bushmen, similarly, moved their homes from place to place in response to the movements of antelope and other game, or according to the availability of such food resources as honey, snakes, flying-ants and birds.

The hunting skills of the Bushmen were quite extraordinary, necessarily so if they were to survive in the harsh environment into which they had been driven. The women and children were responsible for finding edible roots, wild berries and fruits; the men concentrated on game, using bows with poison-tipped arrows. Snares, traps and pitfalls were also employed.

The first waves of invaders came from the North in the form of the Bantu, the Black tribes that had been gradually migrating southward from Central Africa. Most of these Bantu moved down the well-watered eastern seaboard where

Initiation ceremonies for Xhosa Blacks, Eastern Cape

there was good pasture for their cattle. They slowed down as they reached the drier areas just south of the place we now know as East London.

Historians hold differing views on the timing and locations of these early Bantu migrations into South Africa. There is general agreement, however, that four major groups were involved: the Sotho, Nguni, Tsonga, and Venda. The Sotho and Nguni were probably in the vanguard, while the Venda were last to cross the Limpopo River.

Ruins of stone-walled settlements have been unearthed in a wide east-west belt spanning central Transvaal. This belt covers the best grassland pastures of the Transvaal, evidencing selective settlement by the cattle-owning Blacks.

Witch doctors play critical medical roles in Zulu culture

The homes in these settlements belonged to early Sotho tribes.

The Xhosa, a sub-group of the Nguni, who settled in the Southeast, were the first to encounter European settlers. Toward the end of the eighteenth century, these contacts led to frontier wars as both sides fought over land and cattle ownership rights. At first the wars were limited in extent, involving only a small band of settlers who had moved outward from the Cape. By 1820, however, as British settlements appeared on the eastern coast, and European colonization extended farther north, the frontier wars intensified.

The Khoisan were the people who suffered most from the

Black-White conflicts. Caught in the middle, they were out-numbered and conquered. Subsequent archeological re-search has revealed the age and cultural wealth of these orig-inal inhabitants. Cave paintings, which date back many thousands of years, show that aesthetic needs were a high priority, even at that early stage.

Meanwhile, farther north, the immigrant Black communi-ties were experiencing endless conflict over either land and cattle or control of such lucrative routes as the ivory trade into Delagoa Bay. At the beginning of the nineteenth cen-tury, these inter-tribal tensions exploded into general war-fare involving almost all of the Bantu. The name *difaqane*, meaning bands of marauding soldiers, has been given to this chaotic period. Tribes were decimated and scattered. Wholesale destruction was wreaked on most of the newly-occupied areas. It was one of the bloodiest conflicts in the entire history of Africa.[14]

The key actor in this warfare was Shaka, King of the Zulu tribes. His army was better organized than any other, and from 1821 to 1828 he terrorized the whole of Natal and most of both Orange Free State and Transvaal. When, a decade later, Whites from the Cape arrived in this largely depopu-lated area, it was relatively easy for them to claim territory.

Shaka reorganized his soldiers, known as impis, into highly mobile units, able to travel 40 miles in a single day. He established a rigorous rule of celibacy, made general use of the assegai, a dreaded short stabbing spear, provided im-proved shields, and introduced new techniques of warfare such as extensive use of spies and the now familiar scorched-earth policy. In 1828, Shaka was assassinated by his two half-brothers. One of them, Dingane, became the Zulu leader for a further ten years. Not until the 1838 his-toric clash with the voortrekkers, who migrated northward in the Great Trek, was the power of the Zulus finally broken.

In spite of small-scale warfare from time to time, there has been a steady improvement in inter-tribal relations over the past 150 years, partly a result of the balance of power which came with the new migrants from the South, partly due to the reorganization of tribal homelands by the British Colo-nial authorities.

These homelands were not created by the colonial author-ities. Traditionally, each tribe occupied its own area, having boundaries that waxed and waned with conquest and defeat.

Homes were clustered in rural villages. There were customs and a social organization, with a tribal chief as titular head of the community. At no time were they slaves. Their sense of identity and independence was evident in strong resistance, initially, to any form of migration when there were opportunities for work in the towns.

The land allocations that fixed the territorial limits of each tribe were established by the British, and so inter-tribal conflict was largely eliminated. At the same time, arguments erupted over the amounts of land being given. There was good reason for the complaints because, subsequently, additional land was added. However, the idea persisted that Blacks had been penned into tiny enclaves, while Whites inherited vast areas of the country.

What was overlooked in comparing land areas was the agricultural potential of each region. Almost all the tribal lands were located in high rainfall areas. Most of the rest of the country was desert or semi-desert. The allocation to some Tswana tribes, for example, because their homeland was desert, was an area we know today as the nation of Botswana, equal in size to half of South Africa. On the average, the land areas of the present homelands—both self-governing and independent—are greater than those of thirty other world nations.

In other ways, too, the homelands compare favorably with other nations. Graphs for the four independent states, and four African countries with matching populations, show the economic strengths and general living conditions in all eight nations.[15]

A tribe is usually defined as a group of people with a common language, a common set of values, a feeling of kinship, group loyalty, and a high degree of concentration in a specific geographical area. When Blacks from tribal homelands finally began to move to the cities, in response to the job opportunities that came with industrialization, there was an assumption that tribal characteristics had vanished. Everyone now dressed alike, the patterns of tribal authority were removed, and the environments of work and residence looked like those in industrialized societies everywhere.

This was a very superficial interpretation of the nature of cultural mores. They do not change markedly in a few years or even in a few generations. In fact a series of generations is by far the best way to see that cultural characteristics last a

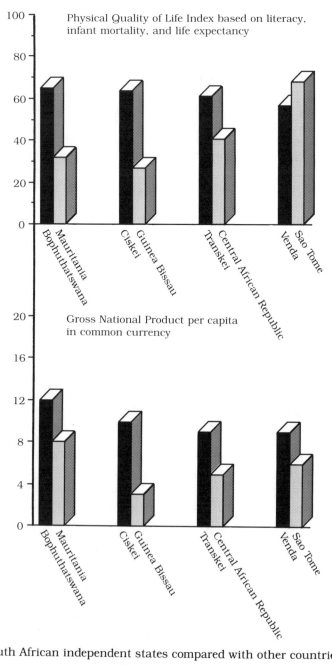

South African independent states compared with other countries

long long time. It requires only three consecutive generations to cover a century of history and bring forward from one age group to another the traditional values and influences of their forebears. The inter-tribal fights so frequently seen in the urban townships of South Africa provide ample evidence of the persistence of ancient attitudes and habits.

At present, ten tribal homelands can be identified on the map of South Africa. In addition there are millions who have migrated from these places and have become permanent residents of the big urban centres—Johannesburg, Durban, Port Elizabeth, and Cape Town. Four of the homelands have chosen independence from South Africa; others are self-governing. At an earlier time, when South Africa was a colony of Britain, today's nations of Swaziland, Lesotho and Botswana were separate homelands. In 1961, South Africa severed its ties with the Commonwealth and became a republic. Soon afterward, Britain granted independence to these three homelands. Now, because of almost universal opposition to South Africa's laws, the world community will not recognize the homelands which have recently been given their independence. South Africa has therefore offered dual citizenship to those of their people who formerly lived in South Africa.

The reason for the world's rejection of the homelands was not their existence as separate entities. That pattern was fully accepted, both in colonial days and in the post-World War II era, just as Indian reservations are a recognized part of North American life. The objectionable features were the laws removing such fundamental human rights as the freedom of a Black to marry a White. Many such laws were passed in the 1950s and 1960s.

Even though these laws have now largely been repealed, they continue to be exploited by revolutionary organizations. Periods of unrest and violence continue to erupt. One of the worst outbursts occurred in 1985 and 1986. The communist-led African National Congress decided to make the country once and for all ungovernable by creating mayhem in the urban townships. A small group of young revolutionaries were encouraged to kill anyone who either advocated a peaceful resolution of grievances, or participated in any way with the normal institutions of society. Within an eighteen-month period, more than 3,000 homes and 1,000 schools were destroyed and about 300 Blacks murdered by the bar-

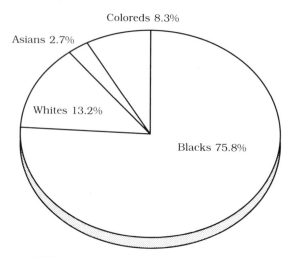

Population 1988
(Total: 37.2 million)

baric necklace method. Intervention by the military, coupled with the establishment of a State of Emergency, brought a quick resolution to the crisis. The persistence of this state of emergency is now the new basis for protest.

With the growth of the South African economy over the past three decades, Black urban townships have seen the emergence of a large, wealthy, middle class. One section of Soweto, the largest of the urban Black residential areas, has been named Beverley Hills, because of its grandiose homes. Increasingly, these upwardly-mobile Blacks are involved in the wider community as lawyers, doctors, engineers, and stockbrokers. The South African Black Taxi Association recently paid US$75 million to take over a White-owned bus company. In the wake of these developments, assisted as they are by the removal of apartheid laws, including the opening to everyone of some formerly Whites-only city suburbs, there is a construction boom underway.[16]

In the rural areas, one interesting development augurs well for the future of Black society. In Gazankulu, one of the poorest areas of the country, as many as 50,000 refugees from Mozambique have been permanently adopted. These refugees, escaping from certain death in their home country, because of either starvation or violence, travelled through Kruger National Park at night, risking encounters with wild animals, in order to reach safety. The people of Gazankulu, a self-governing homeland which borders the Park, have made the newcomers welcome and have readily shared their meagre resources with them. Since they speak the same language as the refugees, the problems of assimilation have been eased.[17]

As part of the process of dismantling apartheid, the government has given new powers and autonomy to the self-governing states. Functions such as planning, development, administration and maintainance of townships, all are examples of the new functions being handed over to local authorities. Meanwhile, in Canada, a 1988 measure of self-government, for one group, has been acclaimed as a breakthrough in native rights, despite the fact that it falls far short of the degree of autonomy given by the South African government to its native peoples.[18]

The following are brief descriptions of the independent and self-governing homelands:

Independent States

Bophuthatswana

Second of the homelands to become independent (1977). Principal tribe is the Tswana. The state is fragmented into seven blocks of land with a total area of 41,000 km². Population (1988): 2.1 million.

Bophuthatswana has three main agricultural zones: the cattle ranching areas of the semi-Kalahari in the west, the mixed farming areas of the east, and the irrigation lands of the south. In addition, the country has great mineral wealth, including the largest platinum mine in the world. Because of their proximity to the industrial heartland around Johannesburg, the Tswana people of Bophuthatswana are more exposed than any other Black group to Western industrial and commercial practices.

Ciskei

Fourth homeland to become independent (1981). Principal tribal group is the Xhosa-speaking South Ngunis. The state has been consolidated into a single land block of 8,000 km^2. Population (1988): 1 million.

The original settlers left the Transkei in the early nineteenth century and crossed the Kei River. Because the people of Ciskei and Transkei belong to the same tribal group, Transkeian leaders feel that Ciskei should be incorporated into their country. Economic resources include a coastal strip which is suitable for fruit and mixed farming, and interior highland areas where stock rearing is the main land use. There are also industrial centres such as Dimbaza.

Transkei

This was the first South African homeland to become independent (1976). There are three land parcels in a total area of 42,000 km^2. Population (1988): 3.6 million.

In the nineteenth century, Transkei was home for the five main Cape Nguni tribes plus the Fingo. This was during the period of British colonial rule. It was incorporated into the Cape Colony in the latter part of the nineteenth century but continued to be administered as a separate region. Xhosa is the most common language. Sugar cane, subtropical fruits, corn, tea and coffee all are grown on the coastal land strip. On the interior plateau there is mixed farming and cattle rearing.

Venda

Third homeland to become independent (1979). Land is consolidated into a single block with a total area of 7,000 km^2. Population (1988): 500,000.

The Vendas are numerically the smallest of the ten Black ethnic groups. They are related, in terms of language, to the Shona of Zimbabwe. A mountain range which runs east to west divides the country into two distinct climatic regions. To the north lies hot, dry, bushland, suitable for extensive ranching. In addition, there are several northward-flowing rivers and these have been harnessed for irrigation. South of the range, mixed farming, corn and vegetables are characteristic farming activities.

Self-Governing States

Gazankulu

Homeland of the Shangaan/Tsonga people, consisting of three land parcels with a total area of 7,000 km². Population (1988): 700,000. Most of the biggest land parcel borders Kruger National Park.

Agriculturally, Gazankulu is mainly a cattle ranching area with some smaller scale activities such as sisal. Some irrigation lands produce corn and cotton. Gold, copper, and zinc minerals are being mined.

KaNgwane

Swazi homeland in two land parcels with a total area of 5,000 km². Population (1988): 600,000.

Because of limited mineral resources and remoteness from large markets and industrial centres, the people of KaNgwane depend almost entirely on agriculture for their economic life. Cattle rearing dominates. In addition, there are some timber resources in the mountain areas.

KwaNdebele

Located in one consolidated land parcel of 3,000 km². Population (1988): 500,000.

KwaNdebele is the last of the homelands to be identified. It was 1980 before it achieved self-governing status. The Ndebele people who live there have come from various parts of the country, including a substantial migration from Bophuthatswana where the Ndebele had experienced discrimination at the hands of the Tswanas. A large proportion of KwaNdebele's working population commute daily to the urban and industrial areas around Pretoria because, as yet, there is little development closer to home.

KwaZulu

This is the Zulu homeland, scattered in ten parcels of land with a total area of 32,000 km². Population (1988): 5.3 million.

A large variety of agricultural products can be grown on KwaZulu's sub-tropical lands. The coastal strip is well-watered and is suitable for sugar cane, bananas, sisal, and pineapples. Grain growing and cattle grazing constitute the principal land uses in the remainder of the territory. There are mineral deposits of coal, copper and nickel and several mines are in operation. Of much greater value, however, is the close proximity of most of KwaZulu to the manufacturing and service regions of Natal where employment opportunities are plentiful.

Lebowa

Homeland of the North Sotho. Consists of six land parcels with a total area of 22,000 km². Population (1988): 2.6 million.

In this northerly part of South Africa water is more plentiful than in most of the country and temperatures are high. The subtropical lowlands are frost-free for eleven months in the year. Coffee and mixed farming are common types of land use. Lebowa also has rich mineral deposits, including chrome and asbestos.

Qwaqwa

South Sotho homeland. Total area of the one consolidated territory is 1,000 km². Population (1988): 500,000.

This is the smallest of the states. It is located on the borders of Lesotho and Natal and consists for the most part of mountainous terrain. The area was originally set aside for two Sotho tribes more than a century ago. The land is largely unsuitable for agriculture and the location is too far from urban and industrial centres for daily commuting to work. Tourism, with emphasis on mountaineering, is seen as one of the best prospects for employment.

In the long history of Black settlement, the transition from tribal warfare to cooperative societies has been a painful and gradual development. Recent constitutional structures for South Africa make provisions for a common citizenship for both self-governing and independent states. However, those that have fared better than others economically stand to lose their higher standards of living in a common political dispensation. Hence, the government now faces the challenging task of bringing these disparate communities together into one federation. If a united, multi-racial democracy is to be achieved within this century, only statesmanship of the highest order will make it possible.

Statue of Paul Kruger, Pretoria

3 | White Africans

The Promised Land always lies on the other side of a wilderness.

Havelock Ellis
The Dance of Life, 1923

Bartolomeu Dias, the Portuguese explorer, was the first European to set foot on South African soil. He landed at Mossel Bay, on the South Coast, in 1488, then went on to the mouth of the Great Fish River, just south of the present site of East London, before returning to Portugal. The 500th anniversary of his epic voyage was commemorated in February of 1988, in the form of a repeat trip from Portugal, using a replica of one of the original caravels. Ten years after Dias, another Portuguese explorer, Vasco da Gama, sailed the same waters and went beyond them to India. However, it was more than another 150 years before Europeans established a permanent settlement in South Africa.

The Dutch who arrived in Cape Town in 1652 were small in numbers. They only wanted to man a supply port in order to victual the ships that plied the trade routes between Europe and the Dutch East Indies. The growth of that supply port into a large farming community, then into a nation of trekkers who moved northward and created new countries out of an inhospitable, thinly-populated, dry, interior, was due to a series of historical accidents. Their lifestyle and attitude to natives were unique in the annals of European-African relations. The administrative structures they employed were fundamentally different from the colonial domination that became characteristic of Europeans in later years.

At their beginning, in Cape Town, the new arrivals bar-

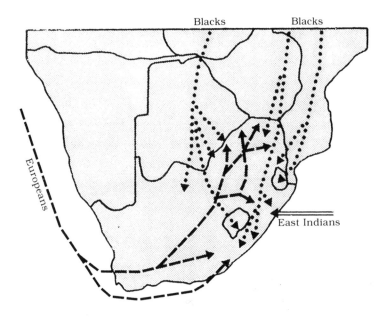

The settlement of South Africa

tered with the native Hottentots for the fresh meat they needed. Fresh vegetables, vital for the prevention of scurvy on long voyages, were grown on the grounds of the settlement. Within a very few years, however, demand outstripped supply. To provide sufficient vegetables, slaves were imported from Java, Madagascar, and Africa to work in the fields. Provision of meat was a bigger problem. The Hottentots had became increasingly disinterested in trade, and reacted violently when the Dutch brought in their own stocks of cattle and sheep. A change of policy was essential, if the settlement was going to meet the growing demand; bartering had to give way to the kind of large-scale farming needed for stock rearing.

After some experimentation, and with permission from Holland, Jan van Riebeeck, the first Governor at the Cape, began cattle farming. He granted freedom, and a certain amount of land, to men who were willing to establish farms, and sell their meat to the Governor at a fixed price. The settlement was now no longer just a staging post or temporary community. The new farmers, known as free burgers since they had obtained their freedom from military duties, had become permanent settlers.

These free burgers soon discovered that there was less and less rainfall as they moved into the interior. Bigger tracts of land were therefore needed to provide pasture for their cattle. Gradually there developed a new kind of farmer, a trekboer, *boer* being the Dutch word for farmer, who wandered far afield in search of adequate pasture. As he moved farther away from the Cape, he became more independent, because the central authority had difficulty exercising its control so far afield.

Developments at the Cape accelerated these moves into the interior by creating more demand for food. Political deportees began to arrive from the Dutch East Indies despite the protests of the Governor that he could not accommodate them. The Dutch government then decided to encourage, rather than just permit people to settle permanently at the Cape. Under this new policy, the first immigrants were Huguenots who fled France to avoid religious persecution. One hundred and fifty of them arrived at Cape Town in 1688.

By the year 1700, the Cape's population of 2,000 occupied an area extending 100 km inland from Table Bay. The Dutch communities of Stellenbosch, Paarl, and Drakenstein date from this period. Similarly, most Huguenots occupied the French settlement of Franschhoek, a Dutch word for French corner. At this stage, the Governor of the Cape settlement still insisted on fixed prices for the main crops of wheat and wine. The trekboers, however, felt that they were working too hard for the profits they received. As a result, farmers shifted to cattle rearing, a method of farming which requires much less capital and labor, but also one which demands large tracts of land.

The trekboer drive for new and bigger pastures led to a huge time gap between the opening up of new farms and the establishment of civil authorities in their respective vicinities. Sometimes the gap was as much as thirty years. During this time the farmers had to fend for themselves, first against the Bushmen and then against the Blacks. Disputes over grazing rights and cattle rustling were the main causes of the fights and wars that ensued. Commando units, volunteer bodies of farmers' militia, were organized for emergency use to fend off the Xhosa Blacks. These commando units were to prove extremely effective in later years during the wars with the British.

It was bad enough that the Governor and his staff at the Cape failed to provide protection for these farmers. To make matters worse, they followed a conciliatory policy toward the Xhosa which was interpreted by the Blacks as support for their rights. By the end of the eighteenth century, trekboer opposition to civil authority had led to open rebellion, followed by attempts to govern themselves.

In 1806, during the Napoleonic wars, the British captured the Cape for the second time; this move marked the beginning of a series of vast colonial conquests across the southern half of the continent. In the years that followed, this colonial empire extended to all of South Africa, Lesotho, Swaziland, Botswana, Zimbabwe, Zambia, Malawi plus other areas farther north. For the trekboers, the change of government was to lead to even more tension with the established authorities.

In an attempt to minimize the fighting between trekboers and Xhosa on the eastern frontier, the British Governor created an agricultural area near the Great Fish River in the hope that it would act as a buffer between the warring factions. Several thousand British settlers were brought in to work the land. This venture met with failure, partly because of the poor soil, partly because of their lack of adequate farming knowledge, and partly because of intermittent attacks from the Xhosa.

The British Governor was anxious to keep the trekboers within the Cape Colony. However, by this time it was obvious that the feeling was not mutual. These frontier farmers were already settling beyond the bounds of the Colony. By 1834, the Great Trek had begun, a major and far-reaching migration that transformed the trekboer into the pioneering voortrekker, the Afrikaans word *voor* meaning in front. This phase marked the coming of age of the Afrikaners, the name adopted by the voortrekkers to distinguish them from the settlers at the Cape. It was to be the only African people named after the continent of Africa. Within a decade, as many as 14,000 of these Afrikaners had settled beyond the boundaries of Cape Province.

The continuing frustration with British authority was

clearly one of the chief reasons for the Great Trek. Many factors gave rise to the growing alienation. When Blacks raided trekboer farms and stole cattle, English authorities demanded part-payment in cattle to defray the costs of recovery, even when the Boer farmers recovered their own stock. The move that finally triggered the exodus to the north, however, was the 1834 edict abolishing slavery throughout the British Empire. Slaves had been sold to the farmers by the English, so financial compensation for the loss of slaves was part of the Emancipation Act. But there was a catch; they could only get their money in England, an arrangement that meant no compensation of any kind.[19] The trekboers departed northward with enough resentment, as one writer pointed out, to last a century. It was to be a little more than a century before they had the opportunity to correct some of these deeply-felt injustices.

South African slavery was never the problem that it was in the U.S. and Caribbean. South Africa had no plantation economy. The maximum number of slaves never exceeded the total White population. The Black tribes that entered the country from the North never were slaves. In addition, from the beginning, the philosophy of the Afrikaners was live-and-let-live. Unlike the European settlers in Australia, Canada, and New Zealand, there was no attempt to destroy the social and economic tribal structures. This is what Piet Retief, an outstanding Afrikaner leader, said in 1837:

> Wherever we go, no one shall be held in a state of slavery. We will not molest any people, nor deprive them of the smallest property. On arriving at the country where we shall permanently reside, we purpose to make known our intentions to the native tribes, and express our desire to live in peace and friendly intercourse with them.[20]

The journey into the unknown was fraught with enormous difficulties. There were differences of opinion among the leaders as to where to go. There was the necessity of keeping all arrangements secret from the British authorities. Fortunately inter-tribal strife had largely depopulated much of the interior and they were able to find adequate pasture. Finally, with due regard to the problems of fighting the Zulus and other tribes further north, they moved eastward and formed their first independent state, Natal. Negotiations with Dingane, the Zulu Chief, led to a series of conflicts culminating in the historic 1838 battle of Blood River, where the Zulus were decisively defeated.[21]

The new voortrekker Natal lasted only four years. The British saw the danger of an independent Afrikaner state with access to the sea at one of South Africa's few good natural harbors. The Governor of the Cape, now Sir George Napier, used the relocation of unsettled Blacks to southern areas as an excuse to annex Natal, arguing that the presence of the Blacks would create friction and violence on the eastern frontier.

Once again the voortrekkers moved away into unknown territory in a second great trek, again in quest of independence from the British authorities. They moved westward and as far north as the Limpopo River, experiencing renewed conflict as they approached the more thickly populated territories of the Ndebele and the Zulus.

The deeply-rooted piety of the Afrikaners, with their loyalty to the Bible, and their expectation of God's guidance in daily life, has often been the subject of ridicule. Writers have implied that they claimed to be God's chosen people, like the Jews in the Old Testament period. The vow of dedication, taken at Blood River, is often cited as evidence of this claim. It is a spurious assertion, one that no serious theologian has ever made. The reality of eighteenth-century Afrikaner life depicts a simple, uneducated people fighting for survival, grasping at every thread of hope in their quest for freedom and safety.

The British, by the middle of the nineteenth century, burdened with the costs of administration, were ready to jettison responsibilities wherever they could, so the Afrikaner drive for independence was almost welcomed. In 1852, the year in which David Livingstone began his cross-Africa exploration of the Zambezi, the Convention of Sand River gave recognition for the first time to an independent voortrekker republic, the Transvaal, or the South African Republic as it was first named. Soon afterward, Orange Free State, which had been settled by the same trekkers and annexed by the British, was added as a second independent voortrekker republic. The Great Trek had come to an end.

Afrikaners could look back on a rich heritage of courage and loyalty, one that would serve as a source of inspiration in times of stress. In the years of sorrow and poverty that followed Boer War II, this heritage became a rallying point, drawing Afrikaners together once again into a new, strong bond of unity. In 1938, at the first centenary of the Battle of Blood River, a symbolic ox-wagon trek was staged, beginning at various points in the country and culminating in Pretoria. Intense emotions swept the nation, especially among the many thousands who attended the climax at Pretoria's Voortrekker Monument. Dr. D. F. Malan's National Party reached a new plateau of popular support.

The eruption of World War II created a hiatus in the new wave of Afrikaner nationalism, but it soon surfaced again and helped the National Party gain power in 1948. Fifty years later, at the 150th anniversary in 1988, the emotive power of Blood River was still evident in a repeat ox-wagon safari. The two leading parties in government, the Nationals and the Conservatives, vied with each other in competing celebrations, each recognizing the political power of the memory and legend of the Great Trek. Despite the passage of time, Afrikaner heritage, as focussed in the events of 1838, has lost none of its power to mould national life.

Opening session of the Tricameral Parliament, 15 January, 1985

4 | Shades of Brown

Purity of race does not exist. Europe is a continent of energetic mongrels.

Herbert A. L. Fisher
A History of Europe, 1934

The people known as Coloreds and Indians, or Asians, as the latter are often called, are anomalies in South African history. They do not represent new settlers in the same way as do Whites and Blacks. Their presence is the result of actions taken by other people. The Coloreds are the offspring of intermarriage between the different races at the Cape; Indians were introduced by the British colonial authorities to work the Natal plantation fields. Both groups share with Whites a number of similarities such as language and political tradition. In recent years these common interests have been expressed in a new constitution which gives Coloreds and Indians a high profile in the central government.[22] By contrast, the Blacks arrived in South Africa independently, and settled in specific geographical locations, with their own political and social structures already in place.

In the early years at the Cape, there were slaves from different parts of Africa, Malays from the East Indies, Hottentots and Bushmen from the immediate hinterland, and Europeans of various nationalities. Illicit intercourse and intermarriage between members of this mixed population led to the Coloreds of today, now numbering close to three million. Traditional practice in the Dutch East Indies had allowed settlers to marry local women. This practice was followed at the Cape for a time and then forbidden in 1682. However, in spite of the prohibition, a great deal of miscegenation persisted.[23]

There are two sub-cultural groups of Coloreds: Griquas and Cape Malays. The Griquas are of Hottentot-European ancestry, and live in the northwestern and northeastern parts of the Cape. Their cultural identity is gradually eroding as they become more and more involved in the larger Colored community. Their langauge, a broken form of Afrikaans, and their characteristic adherence to Christian traditions are assets in the process of assimilation.

The Cape Malays, a small group descended from seventeenth century slaves brought from the Dutch colonies in East Asia, are concentrated in the Cape Peninsula. Their religious tradition is Muslim, a faith they have consistently expressed in their feasts, weddings, funerals, and pilgrimages to Mecca. Originally, as craftsmen and artisans, they provided invaluable skills for the fledgling community in Cape Town. With the growth of industrialization nationally, their craft industries have given way to factory work.

The main group of Coloreds has traditionally been employed in fishing, agriculture and service industries. Recently, this pattern changed, as development created demand for highly-skilled artisan trades in the clothing and construction industries. With the change of work came higher wages. Compulsory education, which was introduced in 1974, contributed substantially to this improvement in standards of living.

The Indians were brought in as indentured laborers and put to work on the sugar plantations of Natal. Their contracts were initially for five years, after which they could either return to India or stay on for a further five years. At the end of a ten year period they had to make a choice: go back to India, fare paid, or stay permanently. Most chose the latter. At a later time, other Indians arrived and settled, not as laborers but as business people. Competition with the Whites ensued, and a number of discriminatory laws were then introduced by White authorities to minimize the threat to their enterprises. This activity peaked after 1948 with the new Group Areas legislation, under which separate residential areas were established for the various minorities. At this time, there was considerable property loss for the Indians, because government, rather than the private sector, decided how much compensation was to be paid. Today the total Indian population is close to one million, their largest single concentration outside of India.[24]

Coloreds and Indians have traditionally been regarded as an intermediate population, a sort of bridge spanning the two poles that so often characterize Black and White relationships. More recently this mythology has been exposed. A project undertaken by the Human Sciences Research Council reveals that the social distance, or the felt differences between Indians and Blacks, are just as great as those between Whites and Blacks.[25]

Political rights for both Indians and Coloreds were not given a great deal of attention in the early years of settlement. A kind of informal right to vote existed, but few took advantage of it. Then in the years following World War II, as a new government took office, the question of political rights became an important issue, especially in the light of homeland and group areas legislation. By this time, the franchise had long been removed from the Indian community. Coloreds, however, were still represented in parliament on a common voters' roll. The abolition of that privilege in 1956 was the move that sparked intense debate over the question of political rights.

The debate concerned more than the franchise. From the time of Union in 1910, Colored people enjoyed a constitutional right to vote, and for many years prior to that date they had held that same right under colonial rule. In 1948, after a slim victory at the polls, the National Party, fearing an alliance between English Whites and the Coloreds, removed the Colored franchise, using unconstitutional means. The government did not have the votes to provide the necessary two-thirds majority required by law, so they made new rules, arguing that a mandate from the people carried more authority than a constitution designed by a colonial power.

A wave of protest spread across the country. Successful appeals to the Supreme Court were countered with new moves by the government until, by 1956, the will of Parliament prevailed. One newspaper insisted that by rejecting the constitution and stifling democracy, the government was opening the door to communism. The protest movement known today as Black Sash emerged out of the struggle for Colored voting rights.

Since 1956, various proposals have been advanced to take the place of the former Colored franchise, and one after another rejected. Finally, in 1977, a government commission recommended separate parliaments for Asians, Coloreds, and Whites. It took an additional seven years before that recommendation was implemented. In 1984, a new constitution was inaugurated. It consisted, in the main, of three separate houses: one for Whites, one for Coloreds, and one for Asians. In the eyes of North Americans and many Europeans, a tricameral parliament of this kind seems unwieldy and totally unnecessary. This is not so in South Africa; in the existing atmosphere of intense ethnic feeling, it is per-

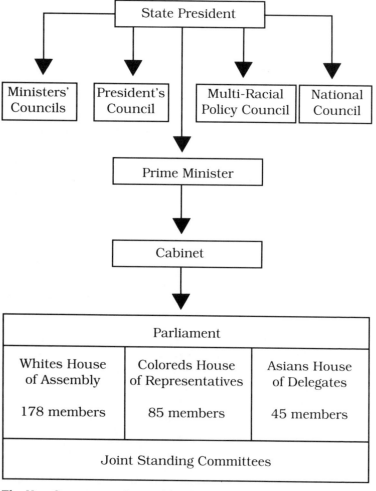

The New Government (central level)

ceived as a necessary, temporary step in the long process of establishing a single parliament.

Today, the three houses practically work as one as members get acquainted with one another. In so doing, a new style of consensus politics is emerging. Legislation is worked out in detail by parliamentary committees, before being presented to Parliament, and Asians, Coloreds, and Whites are all represented on these committees. The nature of the new Parliament requires consensus, not majority vote. If, for any reason, consensus cannot be reached in a particular case, the President's Council is asked for advice or is required to make a decision.[26]

The new Parliament has a House of Assembly for Whites, with 178 members, a House of Representatives for Coloreds, with 85, and a House of Delegates for Asians, with 45. Each house makes laws by majority vote on all matters affecting its own people, for example education and health. The State President is obliged to approve all such legislation. Laws that affect national interests, such as security and foreign affairs, must be approved by all three houses. In the event of disagreement, the President's Council has power to resolve the difficulty. This Council consists of 60 members, most of whom are nominated by the three houses.

Executive authority rests with the State President and his Cabinet together with ministers for national affairs and a ministers' council for each of the three houses. Members of the Cabinet are chosen by the State President from any or all of the three houses, while those in the three councils are identified by their respective houses.

The reality of a working parliament, in which Asians, Coloreds, and Whites share the responsibility of government, is a revolutionary development for South Africa. The long history of Whites-only government has come to an end. The new South Africa has begun to take shape.

Kruger and John Bull, based on an 1899 French cartoon by
Rouville, depicting the Afrikaner and British conflicts

5 | Scourge of War

The two new voortrekker republics, the Transvaal in 1852 and Orange Free State two years later, were a fitting end to the Great Trek. Were it not for the dramatic events of the 1860s, the story might have ended with a "lived happily ever after" postscript; that was not to be. Their biggest problems were yet to come, and they turned out to be far more destructive for the fledgling republics than anything they had experienced in the previous two decades.

In 1867, diamonds were discovered near the borders of Orange Free State. Prospector fever broke out, just as had happened in the earlier gold rushes of the United States, Canada, and Australia. In a few years, thousands of newcomers poured in from all over the world, and, for every new arrival, ten Blacks moved into the Kimberley area from their rural homes. At first the diamonds were mined in the alluvial deposits; then the quest led deep into the earth, into the pipe formations that required large scale machinery and technical knowledge of underground mining. The industry soon passed into the hands of big companies such as the one formed by Cecil Rhodes, the De Beers Company.

A few years after the diamond boom, alluvial gold deposits were found in the Northern Transvaal. By this time, the economic upturn had made South Africa an attractive place for capital investment. Railway tracks began to be laid to the diamond fields from all the main ports: Cape Town, Port Elizabeth, East London, and Durban. Export earnings by the colonial authorities rose to three times the returns they had been receiving from agricultural exports. The growth of South Africa's economy was so great that the opening of the Suez Canal in 1869, with all of its advantages for sea routes to the East, made almost no difference to the volume of sea traffic at the Cape.

There was a much bigger story still to come. For years, prospectors had been searching the Witwatersrand Ridge in the hope of finding a mother lode. They were misled by the dazzling white quartz of the ridge itself, a feature which gave rise to the name, *Witwatersrand*, meaning ridge of white waters in Afrikaans. Mother lode was located some distance south of the ridge and was discovered in 1886. The Johannesburg *Star* described the dramatic find in these words:

> One Sunday in February of 1886, on a farm called Langlaagte, 6 km from the ridge, George Harrison, a stonemason, stumbled on an outcrop of crumbling lichen-speckled rock. He noticed it contained pudding stone, an almost certain sign of gold. Harrison, an old-hand prospector from Australia, crushed a sample, panned it, and saw a glistening tail of gold. He had discovered the Main Reef, a gold reef whose wealth was to excite the imagination of men across the world.[27]

Long before the discovery of these massive underground gold deposits of the Rand, Britain's greedy colonial eyes were fastened on the voortrekker state and its mineral wealth. On the pretext that the Afrikaner republics were not tough enough in their dealings with Blacks, thus risking further Black-White conflict, Britain arbitrarily annexed the Transvaal, then the South African Republic. A further incentive for the British move was the news that the Transvaal was planning to build a railway to Delagoa Bay (now Maputo) in Portuguese Mozambique, and thus obtain independence from the British ports. The smouldering Boer dislike of the British was fanned into flame once more.

Hostilities broke out in 1880, triggered by a small incident involving failure to pay taxes to the British authorities. This first war of independence had a surprising outcome: the British were soundly defeated in a series of encounters. In the final battle, a unit of 500 soldiers was humiliated on Amajuba, a flat-topped, one-mile-high peak. A party of 150 Boers, under cover of diversionary fire, scaled the crags and routed the British, killing 82 men at the cost of only one

casualty. The outcome was the restoration of self-government but not full independence to the Transvaal.

Britain's concession to the Transvaal was a temporary
move. Imperialism was in its heyday and there were dreams
of acquiring more and more colonial territory in Africa. The
prospect of a wealthy, independent Transvaal nation, with
possible rail links to the Indian Ocean, was a serious barrier
to expansion. Two developments heightened Britain's concern: in 1884, Germany surprised the world by annexing a
large part of Southwest Africa, and, in 1886, the discovery of
the reef gold at Johannesburg revealing for the first time the
enormous extent of the Transvaal's wealth.

Britain's plan of action was twofold: first came a series of
moves aimed at encircling the voortrekker republics and
thus controlling their access to the outside world; secondly,
there was the exploitation of imaginary grievances among
the British prospectors who had gone to the Johannesburg
gold fields. Territory to the west of the Transvaal, present-
day Botswana, was taken over, and Zulu lands on the east
were incorporated into Natal. Then the territory to the north,
later known as Rhodesia, was annexed by British interests,
led by Cecil Rhodes.

The prospectors, or *uitlanders* as they were locally called,
had not been given political rights, and the Transvaal government proposed that they wait fourteen years before that
privilege was granted. The British government, seeing its opportunity to contrive a confrontation, insisted on a lesser
time frame. President Paul Kruger, after negotiations, low-
ered the time to seven years, but the British insisted on a
still-shorter time period. It was clear, as Kruger later pointed
out in his memoirs, that the British were determined to gain
full political control of the Transvaal. The seven year concession, had it been accepted, would have ensured a majority
position for as many as 30,000 uitlanders who had been
there for more than seven years.[28]

In 1895, an impatient Rhodes, aided by some friends,
tried to foment a revolution, on the grounds of securing uitlander rights, by staging an invasion of the South African
Republic from territory to the west. The game plan included
priming some of the uitlanders on the Rand to join the invasion forces as soon as they reached the Johannesburg area.
The British High Commissioner was then to be brought in

as arbitrator, in the expectation that the outcome of his intervention would lead to a British bloodless takeover.

The history of nineteenth-century gold rushes in other countries makes it clear that political rights were the least of a gold prospector's interests. The Rand uitlanders were indifferent to the invasion, with the result that the revolution failed, while Jameson, the invasion leader, was arrested. From that moment onward, there was a steady deterioration in relationships between President Kruger and Alfred Milner, the British representative. The fact that the British despised Kruger, because of his lack of formal education and his simple trust in the Bible, accelerated the inevitable confrontation.[29] The stage was set for a second Boer War. Hostilities erupted on 11 October, 1899.

The full extent of the British deceit has gradually come to light over the years. It is now quite clear that there was no enemy and there was no injustice to British subjects. There was only the determination of an imperial power to extend the British Empire no matter what the cost to those who stood in the way. Sir William Butler, who was Acting High Commissioner in South Africa, wrote as follows, in 1898, to the British Secretary for the Colonies: "Nearly all the information sent from Cape Town is false information." For many years, letters such as these seem to have been lost. Not until the publication of Thomas Pakenham's famous 1979 book on the Boer War were the real warmongers finally exposed.[30]

In the ensuing war, an over-confident British Army underestimated the strength of the enemy. Soldiers left Britain in October, 1899, to the cheers of relatives and friends who expected to see them back before Christmas. Within a month, however, the Boers had inflicted such a series of heavy defeats on British forces that the second week of December came to be known as Black Week. Forces were fairly evenly matched at this stage of the War, about 35,000 British to the same number of Boers, or Republicans as they were called. The Republicans stopped at nothing to further their war effort; boys as young as nine fought alongside grandfathers of seventy or more.

Although morale was high among the Republicans, their military equipment failed to arrive in time. Only at the point where war seemed imminent was their order for heavy arms and ammunition sent. Once hostilities erupted, the British prevented deliveries. As ammunition ran out, the Repub-

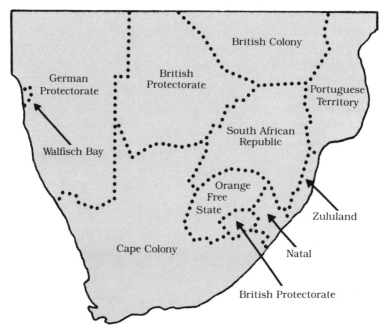

Southern Africa at the outbreak of Boer War II

licans had to rely almost entirely on what they were able to capture from the British. The former's knowledge of the climate and terrain provided an advantage in battle. As expert riders and marksmen, the Republicans formed an ideal, mobile, guerrilla force, compensating in part for their limited firepower.

The problem of shortages in ammunition and guns might never have arisen had not the German Emperor William II made what proved to be an unfortunate move. Shortly before the outbreak of the war, he sent a telegram to President Paul Kruger, congratulating him for his successful handling of the Jameson raid. The British, suspecting that the Afrikaner republics were receiving German support, feared they would have to contend with two enemies in the event of war. They therefore blockaded Delagoa Bay immediately after hostilities broke out, a move they might have avoided were they only to contend with the Afrikaner republics.

Tactically, for the first two months of the war, the Republicans had a slight edge in numbers and a strong position from which to launch attacks. Nevertheless, they blundered badly. Large numbers of troops were deployed to hold locations of minor value such as Mafeking and Kimberley. Worst of all was the decision to take a defensive stance at the beginning of hostilities. For example, they chose not to invade Cape Colony and instead attacked Natal, where the main part of the British garrison was stationed; an invasion at the Cape could have generated a revolt and thereby added to their numbers. Furthermore, the war might well have ended before British reinforcements could arrive.

For four months, in spite of these tactical errors, all of the fighting took place on British territory. General Henry Buller, Commander-In-Chief of the British forces, was repeatedly repulsed in northern Natal with heavy losses. By February, 1900, the British, who now outnumbered the Republicans, began to take the offensive. From that time onward, the Republicans were forced to choose either a defensive position or revert, as they did, to small-scale guerrilla warfare.

Trench warfare was one of the surprises of the conflict. This form of defence, which was to feature so prominently in World War I, totally disrupted British strategy and caused heavy casualties. At Magersfontein Ridge, 3,500 men of Britain's Highland Brigade marched across the plain toward the Ridge, expecting to climb and dislodge the Republicans from the high ground. Instead, they were met with a fusillade from trenches which had been dug at the base of the Ridge. The Highlanders fled in confusion. At the end of the day there were more than 900 British and 200 Republicans dead. It was the second time this method had been successfully employed.

In time, with the steady growth in the colonial forces, to a point where there were four British to one Republican, the tide began to turn. By the end of 1900, because most of the country was under her control, Britain was claiming that the war was over. Unknown at that time were the commando raids, another new and more painful form of warfare that was about to be launched. Like the trench warfare in World War I, these commando raids became familiar in later wars.

The outnumbered Republicans, realizing they could not win by conventional means, spread out in small commando units. They attacked British garrisons across the country in lightning raids that inflicted heavy casualties. The British, in turn, taken aback and frustrated by these events, burned the Republican farms and destroyed crops and animals. This tactic would later be recognized in World War II as the scorched-earth policy of the Russian armies. Republican families were interned in concentration camps. When the scourge of this needless war came to an end in 1902, 30,000 farms lay in ruins, 27,000 Boer women and children had died in the ill-run and unhealthy camps. Republican farmers were so impoverished that they would gladly have sold their farms to Blacks had not the government made it illegal to do so. Deep feelings of anger swept the ranks of the surviving Republicans, scarring Afrikaner-British relations and leaving wounds which have yet to heal.

Detail of a painting of Jan van Riebeeck's arrival in Cape Town

6 | Roots of Apartheid

Culture is not a function of race.

Ruth Benedict
Race: Science and Politics, 1940

The word *apartheid* stands for a whole range of policies, some of which extend back to the original 1652 settlement at the Cape. Apartheid is an Afrikaans word, meaning separate development, and it came into popular usage when the present government, most of whose members speak Afrikaans as their first language, enacted new laws affecting traditional patterns of segregation. Hence, although the word is new, the meaning of apartheid extends far back into earlier history.

Slogans are the staple diets of politicians and demagogues. They provide succinct word pictures that are easily grasped, and that, because of their very brevity and simplicity, inhibit clarity. They can be used to say whatever a speaker wishes to say. Apartheid is a classic example of a good slogan. It is a single, foreign word, belonging to a distant, little-known country. It is easy to give it any desired meaning, because few will be able to question what is said.

Apartheid has been adduced to support the claim that racism, torture, and murder are practiced by the South African government. Consequently, the whole world has reacted with revulsion, treating this nation as a pariah and cutting back on social and economic links. However, the evils in question cannot be equated with apartheid.[31] Indeed, this strange-sounding word from South Africa has sometimes been used to explain the entire set of problems affecting that nation—high population growth rates, water shortages, floods, even the unemployment caused by more than a million illegal immigrants.

From the beginning of European settlement at the Cape, over 300 years ago, the native peoples and other non-Whites lived apart from the Whites.[32] It was a similar story throughout the world in the many places where Europeans took up residence. Cultural disparities were so great that strict segregation was the norm. Two additional factors distinguished South Africa from such countries as Australia, Canada, and New Zealand: the policy of the Afrikaners, who trekked inland in the nineteenth century, included respect for the autonomy and territorial integrity of tribal homelands; the consequence of this was a numerical imbalance in favor of the Blacks, a condition which they used to try to get rid of the White settlers.

The early, informal, patterns of segregation continued into the beginning of the nineteenth century, when the British conquered the Cape settlement and began to administer it as a colony. For the rest of the century, tensions between English and Afrikaner Whites focussed the attention of the colonial authorities, particularly after the discovery of diamonds and gold in the Afrikaner republics. Not until the end of Boer War II, in 1902, when British control was finally imprinted on the whole country, was serious attention paid to the administration of native affairs.

Sir Alfred Milner, British High Commissioner and architect of Boer War II, was determined to make British influence a permanent feature of post-war South Africa. His first move was to encourage large-scale emigration from Britain, so that the English Whites would outnumber the Afrikaners. That move failed. Next, he appointed a Commission, almost all the members of which were English, to deal with native policy. The Commission's report, in 1905, crystallized the informal traditions of segregation in quite a new way.

The territorial separation of Black and White areas was made a permanent feature of land ownership, thus preventing Blacks from buying-up White farms. In the immediate post-war period, many Afrikaner farmers were so impoverished that they had to sell their land, and Black syndicates were ready and able to buy them. By establishing segregated locations for Blacks, both in rural areas and in the urban centres, then tying all federal political rights to the White community, Milner laid the foundations of what we have

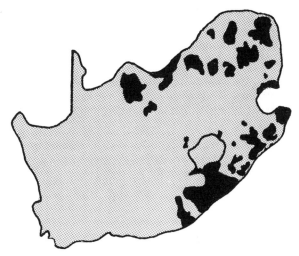

Black states mark the 1850 limits of Black penetration into South Africa

come to know as apartheid. All aspects of his Commission's report were enacted into law long before the present government came to power in 1948.

As was the case with North American Indians, the allocated homelands were those that had been chosen for settlement by the Blacks. These choices were based on two priorities: first, the availability of well-watered land for grazing and hence the concentrations of homelands in the eastern and northeastern sections of the country; second, each tribe's wish to have a buffer strip as a defence against its neighbors.

In 1913, 23 million acres of land were allocated to these homelands as permanent and inalienable Black territory. This was largely the land occupied at the time. In 1917, the emerging vision of the future South Africa was spelled out by General J. C. Smuts, at a London meeting:

> In South Africa you will have, in the long run, large areas cultivated by Blacks and governed by Blacks where they will look after themselves in all their forms of living and development, while in the rest of the country you will have White communities which will govern themselves separately according to accepted European principles.[33]

In 1936, the land allocated to Blacks was increased to 39 million acres, mostly by government purchases from White-owned farms. When the present government came to power in 1948, the apartheid structure, as it is seen today, was already firmly in place.

The legend of vast social changes in South Africa, over the past 40 years, is probably based on the minutiae of what has come to be known as petty apartheid. This refers to the large number of laws that were passed since 1948, restricting movements of Blacks, and establishing separate places and facilities in mixed areas. These petty apartheid laws were sources of enormous frustration and humiliation, probably to a greater extent than were the existing broad structures of grand apartheid. However, their permanent influence on the overall social structure of society, now that they have largely disappeared, has been small.

Hermann Giliomee, the well-known historian from the University of Cape Town, described the long-term effects of the National Party's forty-year rule in this way:

> At the end of his life, Mao Tse-Tung said he was able to change but a few things outside the capital of China. Those who wish to assess the impact of four decades of apartheid on South Africa would do well to consider those words from the man commonly supposed to have shaped modern China.[34]

The 1948 version of apartheid, then, was not something new, only a variety of an old plant, one that had been growing through three centuries of separate living, and one century of formal segregation.

The experiences of World War II, when there was extensive cooperation between Blacks and Whites under the exigencies of war, was clear evidence of the economic value of an integrated society. Sadly, it took more than 30 years to convince the government that it should scrap the laws it had introduced in the early years of its mandate.

These laws appeared as early as one year after the National Party won the 1948 parliamentary election. The Immorality Act modified an older piece of legislation, one which prohibited sexual intercourse between Europeans and Africans, by changing the word Africans to Non-Europeans. A much more difficult piece of legislation was the Population Registration Act, in which every citizen was placed in one of four categories: White, Asian, Black, Colored. It was difficult to define each category in an objective way, because of the long history of marriages and miscegenation across ethnic lines. In many cases, the opinion of a government official had to suffice.

The Group Areas Act refined and reclassified the older patterns of segregation. One of the most painful aspects of this change was the forced removal of people, from so-called White areas, to the places set aside for each group. Many hundreds of thousands were uprooted in this way, some from cities where they had lived for most of their lives. A parallel act, also a refinement of earlier legislation, required Blacks to carry pass books at all times, so that there could be urbanization control. Only those with assured jobs were allowed to stay in the cities.

Population registration, group areas, and the pass books were the pillars of the new apartheid. In addition, there were job reservation laws which excluded Blacks from certain positions in commerce and industry. This development was influenced by the events of the 1920s, when Whites erupted in violence over the loss of jobs to lower-paid Blacks. A new educational structure for Blacks, and a Separate Amenities Act were also introduced in the early years of the new government. The latter detailed a range of separate facilities in parks, toilets, beaches, and transportation systems.

The promotion of the fully-independent Black homelands that Smuts envisioned in 1917 required additional acts of Parliament, and these were enacted in 1970. Powers of self-government, and distinct homeland citizenships, came into force as parts of these new laws. By the beginning of the 1980s, four homelands—Bophuthatswana, Ciskei, Transkei, and Venda—had chosen complete independence from South Africa, while the remaining six opted for various degrees of autonomy in the management of their own affairs.

The concept of totally-separate development became suspect as early as the 1960s. One reason for disillusionment was South Africa's rapid economic growth, which caused business leaders to anticipate a future in which millions of educated, Black workers would be needed in the White areas. By 1978, when P. W. Botha became Prime Minister, there was widespread disillusionment with apartheid, and dismantling had begun.

By the late 1980s, all the legal enactments of the previous 40 years have come under close scrutiny, and most have been scrapped. Milner's hundred-year-old dream vanished into thin air. The stage was set for a brand-new constitution, one that would serve the interests of an integrated and egalitarian society.

Part Two

Contemporary Crises

Urban man is the litmus paper of this great age of transition. The costs of rapid change are etched upon his social relations, his culture and his nervous system. The continuous assault on his senses plays havoc with the mind and emotions. There is a crisis of human identity in cities, inside its value conflicts, its exploitive social institutions, and its alienated individuals.

Thomas Blair
The International Urban Crisis

Crossroads squatter camp near Cape Town

7 | Urban Mecca

*Our education is inadequate, our cities are badly
built, our social arrangements are unsatisfactory.
We can't wait another generation.*

Walter Lippmann

Community life in South Africa's cities is frequently
complex and divisive. In the 1980s, relationships
have been strained by a variety of problems: urbanization, the slowing down of the economy, government
regulations, language barriers, and religious convictions.
There is a deep-felt need for a more cohesive society.

Urbanization has posed the biggest challenge to human
relations. Large numbers have been moving to the cities, especially to Johannesburg, in the wake of industrialization
and, more recently, because of the drought of the early
1980s. These migrants come from all sorts of cultural backgrounds into an entirely new setting. Young people, traditionally related to their elders within a strong hierarchical
system, now find themselves on their own. They acquire a
language and a lifestyle which are foreign to rural areas,
making them feel ashamed of, and estranged from their families.

Over the past 40 years, this kind of steady drift to the cities
has been a worldwide phenomenon. One of the main causes
was the improvement in health services in the 1950s, which
led to rapid increases in village populations. The small landholdings could no longer support everyone, forcing many
young people to move away. Costly attempts by governments
to decentralize the economy, by moving industry to rural
areas, failed to resolve the problem.

In the early 1980s, when a slow-down in the world economy hit South Africa, gold prices, which had risen to unprecedented heights in the 1970s, fell by 60 percent. Worse still was the plummetting of the monetary unit, the Rand, from par to less than US$0.40. Unemployment rose, not only for the new urban dwellers but also for the many immigrants from neighboring countries. The stage was set for unrest and for exploitation of grievances, by political agitators, who had other goals in mind than the elimination of unemployment.

In many cases, crime is the motive behind violent behavior. In rural areas, people know one another, and it is not easy to get away with anti-social behavior. It is quite a different story in the anonymity of the big city. Credo Mutwa, a Black witch doctor who lived in Soweto, points out that our preoccupation with Black-White tensions blinds us to the much more serious problems of Black-on-Black violence. Here is what he said:

> Black people are cruel toward one another in the course of their daily existence in the cities and townships. In one year alone, from 1982 to 1983, an incredible total of 2,475 people were murdered in Soweto. Statistics for subsequent years reveal even worse conditions. These were 'ordinary' street murders, not politically-inspired. They are not something for which the White man can be conveniently blamed, as is always the case when things go wrong in the Black communities....White on Black apartheid has resulted in a lot of suffering and a few thousand deaths in the last forty years; but Black on Black apartheid has claimed the lives of millions and has caused untold suffering.[35]

Traditionally, a system of influx control keeps the numbers entering urban townships at a manageable level. This control has avoided, for the most part, the problems which plague other African cities, creating the kinds of extreme hardships experienced by Ghanians in Nigeria and slum dwellers in Zimbabwe. Yet even with influx restrictions, the problems facing South Africa's urban authorities are immense. It has been estimated that a million Blacks will be added every year for the rest of this century, a growth created mainly by those already living in the cities. Housing, water, and other services will be needed for these people.

Unlike world urbanization in general, South Africa's experience is complicated by two additional factors: there are many thousands of workers who come from rural areas for a year, to work in the mines, and then return to their homes;

In an attack on illegal squatters near Soweto, a Black policeman hurls a woman to the ground

employment is extremely high. They may stay for several years, but will eventually return home. The cities must therefore provide both permanent and temporary accommodations.

The men who come from other countries, such as Lesotho, Swaziland, Botswana, and Mozambique, are interested in more than the job opportunities. They want the social safety net plus the health and welfare provisions that South Africa has to offer. Desperation in the search for better living conditions forces some to risk entering the country illegally.

One attractive aspect of this safety net is the extremely low cost and fully adequate medical provision for Blacks. Urban residents, without regard to their population category, have outstanding facilities which offer preventive and rehabilitative services as well as the usual curative provisions. Baragwanath, Soweto's main hospital and Africa's biggest, is a good example of the quality of care available. It has a large and varied team of world-class specialists, 2,000 beds, 600 doctors, and a large intensive care unit.

In 1967, the country's reputation as a leader in the field of medicine received fresh acclaim when Dr. Christiaan Barnard performed the world's first heart transplant. The patient, Louis Washkansky, died 18 days later, due to a lung infection, but a breakthrough had been made. In the years that followed, similar transplants in other countries have extended the lives of many people.

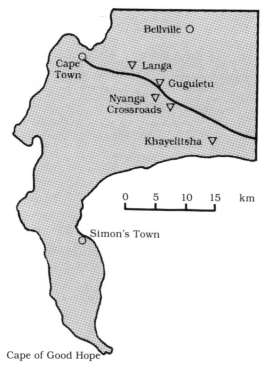

Cape Town and the Cape Peninsula

South Africa's hospitals and specialized medical services are well-known in other parts of the continent. While Baragwanath is designed to serve the 1.5 million residents of Soweto and surrounding areas, the hospital regularly caters to large numbers of patients from such neighboring countries as Swaziland and Botswana. The favorable ratio of 4.5 beds per 1,000 Blacks is another factor in attracting foreign patients. In Africa as a whole the ratio is 2 per 1,000.

In most parts of North America, hospital care is restricted to those who can pay. Seriously-ill patients are regularly turned away from hospital emergency units simply because they cannot afford the fees. Exceptions are made only under extreme circumstances, when survival is at stake. In South Africa, no one is ever turned away. Costs are levied on the basis of an individual's income; hence, in cases of penury, all medical services are free.

The ratio of doctors to patients in South Africa is six times better than anywhere else on the continent. However, there is an unacceptable shortage of Black doctors in the country, a consequence of neglecting Black tertiary education for decades. In the mid-1970s, the three universities with medical faculties (Cape, Natal, and Witwatersrand) graduated only 25 Black doctors annually. However, in 1976, the Medical University of South Africa (MEDUNSA) opened. Today it is graduating hundreds of non-Whites annually.

Crossroads, a squatter camp on the outskirts of Cape Town, is a good example of the problems of South Africa's urbanization explosion. Before the 1970s, when apartheid was being strictly enforced, many immigrants from the Eastern Cape defied the law, and settled at this camp, putting up all kinds of shelters wherever space could be found.

By the early 1980s, during the drought, many thousands more had poured into Crossroads. The haphazard, and sometimes intentional, arrangement of houses and shelters, denied cars and ambulances the needed access to people in times of emergency. The lack of services such as medical care, water supply, and sewage disposal, led to outbreaks of disease, and a deteriorating environment, which could only be described as unremitting squalor. Worst of all, power groups within the camp took advantage of the absence of law and order, to wreak havoc on the defenceless squatters.

Government response was threefold: stop further illegal settlement, help those who are already there to find jobs, and start a new town with adequate services. This response represents a fundamental departure from the long history of completely separate development. Blacks living in urban townships had hitherto been treated as temporary residents, to be permanently settled in their respective states at a later date. Now, instead, they would be given permanent residence and freehold rights in so-called White areas.

Khayelitsha, a Xhosa word meaning 'new home', is the name of the town replacing part of Crossroads. It occupies an eight-thousand acre tract bordering the ocean, less than ten miles from the main employment centres of Cape Town. The design calls for four new towns in Khayelitsha, with accommodation for 250,000. Occupants of Crossroads and other squatter camps are encouraged to move into the new community to permit the upgrading of the old camps.

The services provided for Khayelitsha include tarred roads, sewage disposal, stormwater drainage, high-mast lighting, electricity, and telephone ducts to central locations. In addition, sites are provided for recreation, churches, schools, post offices, community halls, and stores.

There is an unavoidable problem of cost in any venture of this scale. Like third-world migrants in other countries, Crossroads residents have scant resources. Most of them cannot buy their homes. For those who can, there are minimum-size dwellings available; for others sites and services are provided.

The minimum-size homes have two rooms plus tap water and flush toilets. Occupants can expand the premises as they wish. Advice is available for these building extensions. The sites and services are like the basic facilities provided in new subdivisions in North America. The occupants of the sites can install any kind of temporary shelter they desire and improve it as they are able.

Statistical data on Crossroads, like the rest of South Africa, are often confusing because several organizations are involved. For example, South Africa does not include the four independent countries within its borders (Transkei, Bophuthatswana, Venda, and Ciskei) in its official statistics, yet many of the residents of Crossroads have come from Ciskei. Because these four countries are not yet recognized internationally, the rest of the world includes their population numbers in the South African total.

Thus, the estimated total for 1988, given by international

agencies, is 37.2 million, the same figure obtained by adding those for the four independent countries to the national total given by the South African government.[36] In this book all statistical tables or graphs will include the data from the four independent countries.

Large urban centers have become a major feature of population distribution. More than 10 million are now living in the four biggest metropolitan areas: Pretoria-Witwatersrand-Vereeniging (PWV), Durban-Pinetown-Pietermaritzburg, Port Elizabeth-Uitenhage, and Greater Cape Town. Nationally, the concentration of population is in the East, a legacy of early days when agriculture was the principal source of livelihood; only in these eastern areas of the country is an adequate rainfall assured.

In these large metropolitan areas, there are many things that attract people from the countryside: educational opportunities, health services, sports, and various recreational facilities all provide greater scope for the young. Furthermore, even unqualified people can find work in the informal sectors. These "pull" factors are often the main reasons for ambitious, bright people forsaking their rural roots and moving to the city. For others, the "push" factor may be dominant, the quest for survival when there are insufficient resources on the land. In either case, it is the ablest and youngest who migrate, leaving the older folk to eke out a living as best they can.

For industry and commerce, urbanization carries additional advantages, by adding to the availability and mobility of workers. At the present time, most of the Blacks who commute to work from outlying areas, spend as much as four hours daily just getting to work. Additionally, the bus routes determine where they can go, so construction sites are often tied to transportation corridors. Rarely is such an arrangement optimum from a planning perspective.

The rush to the cities by people who speak many different languages creates an additional source of tensions and conflicts. Canadian experience is full of misunderstandings between French and English communities simply because one side lacked language competence in the other. In the United States, Spanish-speakers in New York, Florida, Texas, and California, suffered because they did not know the country's national language.

If differences cause confusion where there are only two,

the problems of South Africa's twenty-four languages can only be imagined. Some of these are so very distinctive in basic structure that special learning approaches have to be developed. A recent survey revealed that large numbers of people had little contact with one another simply because of language barriers.

Very few Asians, Whites, or Coloreds speak any of the languages of the Blacks. In addition, there are serious communication problems among the different tribal groupings. These difficulties are highlighted in the cities. In a typical metropolitan township, only two-thirds of the Blacks speak either of the two official languages. Among the younger ones the proportion is less.

To ensure safety in the mines, a pidgin language known as Fanakalo has been created. It is based on words taken from Zulu, English and Afrikaans. It has a very limited grammar and vocabulary, but it is essential for accurate communications underground where misunderstandings could be disastrous. Newcomers quickly gain a working knowledge of Fanakalo.

Most South Africans are Bantu. Their languages can be subdivided into four main groups: Nguni, Sotho, Tsonga, and Venda. Within each of these four groups there are many smaller language clusters, each being very different from the others. The biggest group is Nguni; it includes Swazi, Zulu and Xhosa. Here are some Zulu words: *umxoxi (The Chronicler)* and *inhlabamkhosi (The Clarion Call)*. These are names of journals published by a Black organization called Inkatha whose President, Chief Mangosuthu Buthelezi, is a Zulu. Asian languages pose a special problem for people from other cultures since they are written in a script that is fundamentally different from Western alphabets.

Differences within the White community are small compared with those between Blacks and Whites or between Asians and either Blacks or Whites. For the most part, they amount to small differences between the two official languages, Afrikaans and English. The Afrikaans word for South Africa, for example, is *Suid-Afrika*.

Afrikaans has an interesting history. It began as Dutch, in 1652, with the first settlers at the Cape. Gradually, among the generations that followed, new words from later immigrants entered the language of the settlers. By the year 1800, Afrikaans was appearing frequently in publications. The years of isolation from its Dutch origins, coupled with the movement of settlers into the interior of South Africa, had created a common language for the various nationalities that now occupied the country.

The drive to the cities will remain a dominant feature of South African life for the rest of this century, and the demand for housing and health a relentless challenge to the authorities. The stresses in human relations are added strains on the social fabric. However, urbanization offers many advantages: access to educational institutions, new opportunities in work and business, and the abolition of social barriers. Urbanization thus provides a long-sought window of opportunity and carries for Blacks the promise of greater freedom and higher standards of living.

In the face of worldwide economic sanctions, the Republic of South Africa's official coat of arms still reads *Union Makes Strength*

8 | Sanctions: The Morality of Hypocrisy

Distrust all in whom the impulse to punish is powerful.

Friedrich Nietzche
Thus Spake Zarathustra, 1891

The quest for good international relations has been the cornerstone of South Africa's foreign policy, particularly in relation to the rest of Africa. Although most of the country's trade and finance are tied to Europe and North America, South Africa sees itself primarily as an African nation.

During the colonial period of its history, when the British Empire stretched from the Cape to the Mediterranean, a large number of transportation, technical cooperation, trade, energy and tourism links were established throughout the southern part of the continent. The railways that were built during that period are a good example of the continuity of those early ties. Most of the overseas trade of Zimbabwe, Zambia and others is still carried on South African rails.

In the 1960s, as European nations scrambled to relinquish their colonies, a wave of pan-Africanism swept the continent, seeking to create a Black identity rooted in the idea of liberation from centuries of slavery and oppression. This concept did not last, because there was too much variety in the new political structures; as one after another of the colonial domains vanished, South Africa came to be regarded as the last White stronghold, a symbol of all past problems.

It did not seem to matter that South Africa was not a colonial territory, or in fact that it was one of the earliest African colonies to be liberated. The presence of a White government, whose forebears had employed slavery, the continuing colonial control over Namibia and, most of all, the policy of apartheid, were sufficient to make it the enemy of Black Africa.

Over the past three decades, these attitudes have set South Africa on a collision course with the rest of the world. The fact that the word 'apartheid' has been officially dropped in South Africa, because the label has mistakenly come to mean racism, does not prevent its retention in other nations.

The imposition of sanctions is particularly confusing to South Africans. Such an action by a Soviet-led group of countries would be understandable, since sanctions cause disruption of an economy, with accompanying unemployment and unrest. The Soviet Union, however, is the least vocal of the world's pro-sanctions nations. It is the Western democracies which are trying to cripple the economy of the nation, despite the fact that their moves are opposed by the majority of South Africa's Blacks.[37]

Chief Mangosuthu G. Buthelezi, leader of the most influential South African Black group, the Zulus, has made it clear that sanctions make sense only if you wish to destroy a country and cause enormous suffering to the people. During the 1988 sanctions debate in the U.S. Congress, a South African delegation, representing 45,000 Black businessmen, pointed out that money and a strong economy are far more powerful weapons against apartheid than sanctions and political rhetoric. Botswana, representing the nations bordering South Africa, made a similar presentation to the U.S. Congress, reminding them that trade embargoes against South Africa have devastating consequences for all of Southern Africa.[38]

No supplier of goods and services can afford to discriminate against South African Blacks when they have substantial buying power. The free enterprise marketplace thus erodes the barriers of apartheid, just as Merle Lipton predicted it would in her mammoth book on capitalism and apartheid and, more recently, in *Sanctions and South Africa*.[39] Today, in the wealthier Black areas of the country, there is hardly a restaurant, hotel, or sporting facility that remains segregated.

Western actions often heighten the confusion surrounding sanctions. Late in November, 1986, the Canadian Minister for External Affairs removed the restrictions imposed on the Soviet Union when it invaded Afghanistan. The reason for the change of policy was that the sanctions had been ineffective; however, this was entirely predictable.

Historically, economic sanctions have rarely achieved their intended purposes. One reason for their failure is the willingness of some nations to take advantage of trade opportunities so long as the price is right. A second explanation is the reaction of the victimized country. When trade measures against Italy were taken in the Abyssinian crisis of 1935, Italy's economy suffered, but the Abyssinians continued to die; in fact, Italy's control over that country was intensified. U.S. sanctions against Cuba impoverished that island nation but, by driving it into the arms of the Soviet Union, the West succeeded in making Fidel Castro one of Latin America's strongest leaders.

Similarly, in South Africa, sanctions have had the opposite effects to those intended. Unemployment has increased, while the reform process has been impeded by a political shift to the right, toward maintenance of segregation. Western companies operating in the country have long been under obligation to assist in the upgrading of health and social services in the poorer areas. They also are under pressure to increase their numbers of non-White executives. When international lobby groups force these companies to leave, the new owners are free to discard traditional social obligations.

When General Motors Corporation decided to leave South Africa, the new owners, Delta Motors, immediately fired 500 workers and dropped off the Sullivan list. This list is named after Leon Sullivan, a clergyman who instituted a code for U.S. companies operating in South Africa, whereby a certain proportion of all profits is devoted to social welfare. Furthermore, the new company reversed the former policy of accelerating the advancement of non-Whites to management positions.[40]

The question arises as to why nations persist with the sanctions method in the face of so many failures. A closer look at Canada's approach to South Africa helps to provide an answer. During the time that gold, in the form of Krugerrands, was banned, sales of Canada's gold coin, the Maple Leaf, soared. Diamonds, which do not compete with any comparable Canadian product, were not included in the ban. South African airlines were forbidden to use Canadian air space, but their planes could be sold to Canadian airlines because the prices were attractive. The list of exceptions goes on: ferrochromium, ferromanganese, and various platinum-group metals all continue to be imported because Canada has no other convenient supplier for these raw materials.

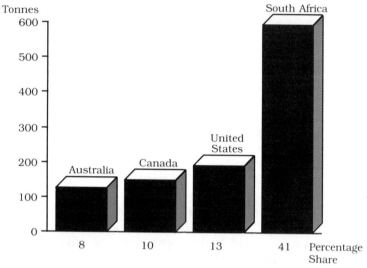

A comparison of the Western world's main gold producers reveals the boost which sanctions give to Canada's economy

It soon becomes clear that sanctions serve very different purposes than those proclaimed. They act as convenient tariff measures when international obligations make it difficult to introduce the usual kinds of trade restrictions. They also serve, in the case of the U.S., to garner Black votes in federal elections. More broadly, they provide low-cost techniques for showing friendship toward other countries. In Canada's case, they help to strengthen ties with African nations.

The evidence for hypocrisy is further strengthened when the so-called desired changes take place. Sport is a good example. A successful boycott was launched against South Africa because its teams were not open to all races. When the changes were made and sporting events were open to all, those who had initiated the boycott changed the criteria and stiffened the demand. They declared that normal sport could not be carried on in an 'abnormal' society.

Multi-racial sporting event

Experiences like these make South Africans wonder what will be necessary to meet the demand for change. At what point in the long process of removing racial discrimination will the advocates of sanctions consider that their objective has been achieved so that the punitive measures can be abandoned? Are they to be maintained until the last vestige of prejudice has disappeared?

Discrimination on the grounds of race and color can be removed from the law books in a moment, as has already been done in South Africa. The elimination of attitudes on the part of Whites, Blacks and others is a very different and much longer process. In the United States today, long after discriminatory laws have been removed from the statute books, old attitudes toward Blacks are still in place.

Unfortunately, just as the slogan of sanctions is a cover for other objectives, so the campaign to eliminate racial discrimination is often a front for a very different goal. The aim of some anti-apartheid organizations is the replacement of the existing order by a majority Black, socialist government. For South Africans, with the evidence of so many African countries before them, the notion that a Black socialist government would be beneficial is far from convincing. They have seen the frequency with which so-called liberation governments change into tribal or military dictatorships.

African countries have had sufficient voting power to influence United Nations resolutions. They have successfully obtained UN condemnation of South Africa for various alleged offences, and they have backed an intensive campaign to interfere with the existing government, irrespective of the tactics employed.

It is quite unfair that African countries should abuse their power at the UN, an institution that is dedicated to the abolition of dictatorial power in the solution of world problems. To give equal voting rights to Botswana or Swaziland, each with less than a million people, and China, with a billion, requires great care and wisdom on the part of each member. Otherwise, one or two small regional groups of countries can outvote the rest of the world. In the case of Africa, this one continent carries a third of the UN's voting power, yet it represents only one tenth of the world's population. In addition, its financial contribution to the operation of the world body is less than 1 percent of operating costs.

One of the most intriguing aspects of Western behavior is the cynicism it elicits from communists. The free nations of the world may not know what they are doing when they blunder into the complexity of South Africa's social world. The communists do. They have taken the time and trouble to find out. A senior ANC leader recently told a Western news correspondent that he could not understand the goals of the West. It appeared to him that Western nations were asking President Botha to eliminate apartheid without telling him what they wanted in its place. The same leader pointed out the problems faced by the ANC: their inability, with their present level of competence, to run the country if they should be called upon to do so.

Against the mindless rhetoric and actions of sanctions, the South African government has consistently held to the high ground, declaring that it will not respond with counter sanctions. It would be easy to withhold vital minerals from the West if it chose to do so. Not everyone is happy with this government position. Early in 1988, a new proposal was advocated by Donald de Kieffer, a well-known South African economist. "Since the U.S. has broken several international treaties in its sanctions drive, why shouldn't South Africa respond by ignoring Western rules on trademarks, copyrights, and patents?", he points out. "Black employee-owned companies could create enormous wealth", says Kieffer, "by churning out IBM software, Levi jeans, Kodak film, videotapes, and textbooks, and selling them throughout Africa at prices Africa can afford."[41]

A critical element remains elusive in all the talk and advocacy of sanctions against South Africa: the absence of a clear statement as to desired outcomes. The explanation for this vagueness may be less confusing; the countries of the West have a multiplicity of purposes in imposing economic hardship on South Africa. Because they are unwilling to reveal their true aims, stated objectives are usually couched in strident pronouncements of an ethical nature. Seemingly, the hypocrisy of sanctions will always be cloaked with morality.

South Africa's Western Deep Levels gold mine. At two and one half miles down, it is the world's deepest

9 | Gold: Engine of Growth

*I am the people. . . . All the great work of the world is
done through me.*

Carl Sandburg
I Am the People, 1916

South Africa has the biggest and most varied manufacturing economy in all of Africa. While most of its
production is destined for the domestic market, the
result of a drive for self-sufficiency, few countries of the
world are unaffected by the country's extensive, highly specialized trade in precious metals. Typically, South African
gold has been the world's safety net when major currencies
falter.

For more than two hundred years, almost every South African depended on farming for a livelihood. Then, in the second half of the nineteenth century, profound changes transformed life for the vast majority, and agriculture became a
minor contributor to the national wealth; yet, despite severe
environmental limitations, and a reduced dependence on its
output, the agricultural sector maintained high produc-
tivity, providing national self-sufficiency in food, and a surplus for export to impoverished neighbors. Furthermore,
many specialized products, such as wine, sugar, and
groundnuts, have been developed to the point where they
provide raw materials for a wide range of manufactures.

Modern industrial societies have always been built on a
strong agricultural base. The replacement of farm workers
by mechanization, and the development of highly specialized, capital-intensive crops, often provided surplus labor for
the factories. In the case of South Africa, industrial labor has
never been in short supply, because of the large numbers of
workers who come from neighboring countries. Neverthe-

less, the agricultural sector has continued to modernize, without regard to labor costs. The present pattern is a model for all of Africa, where farming is frequently in disarray, due to preoccupation with unrealistic political philosophies. Tanzania and Mozambique are examples of countries that experienced serious food shortages because of poor husbandry.

South Africa's landforms and climate are far from ideal for agriculture. It is to the credit of the farmers that they have been successful in the light of these conditions. On the plateau areas of savannah grassland or scrub steppe, where there is a high population density, severe soil and wind erosion pose a serious threat. As early as 1920, General Jan Smuts pointed out that soil erosion is a far bigger issue than politics. One ecologist described this area as having the worst soil in Africa. This is not a recent development but rather the inevitable result of low and unpredictable rainfall in a hot climate. Over one hundred years ago, the voortrekkers noticed that vast quantities of soil were being carried away by water.

The land rises gradually from the West Coast in a series of steep-sided plateaus and mountains toward the centre of the country. In the East, at the highest point, stand the Drakensberg Range, a formidable barrier reaching heights of more than 10,000 feet. The extreme southern part of the

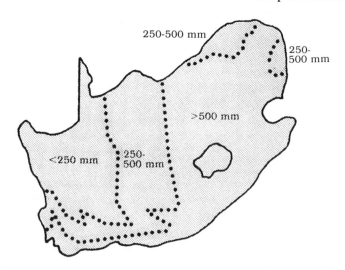

Average annual rainfall

country consists of parallel mountain ranges rising north-ward from Cape Town to elevations of 6,000 feet. Within these ranges there are closed basins, the Great and Little Karoo.

Because the interior areas of the country are dry, stock farming is widespread. Sheep rearing is concentrated in the Karoo regions, and here there has developed an interesting fusion of the two kinds of agriculture found in South Africa, the commercially-oriented sector, mostly in the rural White areas, and the subsistence lifestyles of most of the rural Black homelands. Some business entrepreneurs launched a labor-intensive, wool and mohair, spinning and weaving fac-

Small-scale industry is typified by a weaver at work, Southern Cape

tory, in the Karoo. Mohair is a valuable wool from angora goats, which, after weaving, is much prized on international markets.

The White business people who set up the factory provide the operating expertise, research capacity, and marketing skills needed for success. Because the factory is labor-intensive, it meets the demands of a nation that is part first world and part third. The whole operation fits the description of appropriate third-world technology, the kind that is easy to use and maintain, but requires a large labor force. In Western societies, because labor is so expensive, appropriate technology means capital-intensive industries, with a minimal work force.

In the Black urban townships, the equivalent appropriate technology is the informal sector. Here, street vendors sell everything from fresh fruit to hamburgers, from shoelaces to watches. They may have regular jobs alongside these free-lance ventures, or they may be unemployed. The products may have been purchased directly from farms, or they may have come from other informal, sub-contracts, such as knitting and sewing circles in private homes. The variety of products and services offered in these ways is endless, and their gross value has been estimated at US$10 billion annually, about one quarter of the total South African GNP.[42]

South Africa is an ideal setting for the informal sector. Services for the wealthier members of the community can be provided at low cost while, at the same time, the unemployed can enter the labor force in hundreds of ways. In addition, workers who want to supplement their income in their spare time can do so.

Soweto and Johannesburg are good examples of the informal sector in action. While Blacks are the main entrepreneurs, there is a large minority of Whites whose activities outside their main employment never feature in the national statistics of wealth. Chartered accountants and architects repair cars or make furniture and sell their skills or products in the underground economy. Wives spend their afternoons baking or embroidering for weekend sales at neighborhood markets.

In Soweto there are scores of painters, plumbers, and electricians ready to work at any hour, provided they are paid in cash and the work is not reported. The total value of this South African underground economy is enormous; consequently, the government is often tempted to put it on a proper business footing and thereby collect revenue. However, the loss of very small enterprises, which would undoubtedly happen if there had to be registration, offsets the value of any revenue collected. Furthermore, despite serious levels of unemployment resulting from sanctions, the informal sector provides a small income for many and reduces the risk of riots.

There is yet another positive facet of this kind of economy. Under the pressure of sanctions, South Africa will likely suffer still higher levels of unemployment within the present labor force, quite apart from the additional numbers entering the work force annually. Private initiatives of the kind seen in the informal sector will provide the leadership needed to create new wealth. Like other beleaguered nations in the past when faced with crises, South Africa can find a solution by exploiting the free enterprise experiences of its people.

Most of the country lies within the subtropical zone of the southern hemisphere. Generally, in these lands, climatic variations are based on latitude, as is the case in African areas north of the equator. In South Africa, however, things are different; other factors, primarily longitude, have become determinants. Three elements are responsible for this unusual pattern: proximity to moist ocean winds, the warm Agulhas ocean current on the east coast, and the cold Benguela in the west.

In the southern winter, April to October, the Cape is the recipient of rain from the westerly winds of the temperate zone. From November to March, in the summer, the southeast winds from the Indian Ocean bring heavy rain to the eastern mountains. These winds lose their moisture as they move farther inland, creating a large dry area in the central part of the country.

The two main ocean currents reinforce the concentration of rain in the east. The cold Benguela reduces temperatures by several degrees, thus lowering rainfall, while the warm Agulhas has the opposite effect. Average precipitation, nationally, is less than 16 inches a year. There are no snow-capped peaks, great lakes or underground reservoirs to be tapped in times of drought. That is a serious limitation in a part of the world that not only has low rainfall but cannot depend on a consistent supply from year to year.

Two tragic anomalies of the 1980s brought home to South Africans the seriousness of an unpredictable climate. Both of these events caused extensive damage to the nation's economy. They provided convincing evidence of the interdependence of agriculture and industry in any developed country. Early in the decade, a severe drought hit the country, forcing many farmers into bankruptcy and, at the same time, lowering the water table. It takes years of substantial rainfall to replace water that is lost in this way.

Soon after the drought, catastrophic floods struck Natal and several inland areas. They were the worst of their kind in living memory. More than 300 people died, half a million were made homeless, and property losses reached US$500 million before the rampaging waters subsided. A low rainfall regime means that there is little vegetation to absorb surface water. This condition, combined with steep terrain, resulted in the loss of topsoil on hundreds of thousands of acres of valuable farmland.

The heaviest rainfall occurs in the rural east where the vast majority of the population used to live. Now, with rapid urbanization and industrialization, the water needs of cities like Johannesburg greatly exceeds the supply. Water demand is growing at a rate of 3 percent a year, yet the available supply is barely adequate to meet present requirements. If the flow of people into urban areas is wisely managed, costs of piping water over great distances can be met. If the country's economy is strengthened, desalination can be as feasible as it is in the desert regions of the Gulf oil states. Water conservation therefore requires long-term planning under circumstances of sustained economic growth. One such plan is the multi-billion dollar Lesotho Highlands Water Project.

With large-scale gold and diamond mining, cities grew rapidly, attracting to their mines and industries large numbers of Blacks from the rural areas. Johannesburg, due to its gold mines and proximity to the coal deposits at Boksburg and Witbank, became the country's largest urban and industrial centre. For a time, manufacturing was limited to the development of a transportation infrastructure. Almost half of today's railway lines were laid prior to 1920, and primary industries continued to dominate the national economy. Only after World War II did manufacturing begin to surpass the combined contribution to GNP of mining and agriculture. At

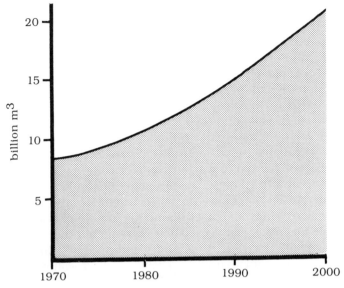

Water consumption trends

the present time manufacturing contributes a quarter of the GNP.

The country's top exports, imports, and trading partners, in order of value, are as follows:

	EXPORTS	IMPORTS	TRADING PARTNERS
1.	Gold	Machinery	United States
2.	Metal products	Manufactures	Japan
3.	Foodstuffs/Fruit	Motor Vehicles	West Germany
4.	Diamonds	Chemicals	Britain
5.	Metal Ores	Metal products	Switzerland
6.	Chemicals	Food	Italy
7.	Machinery	Raw Materials	France
8.	Wool	Textiles	African nations

The Blacks who came to work in the industrial heartland around Johannesburg accurately described it as *Egoli*, place of gold. More than anything else, this precious metal has been the source of the region's and the country's wealth and industrial development. Today, after more than one hundred years of mining, gold still dominates the export trade. The total amount extracted to date equals a third of all the world's gold ever mined; incredibly, though, the country still holds one half of all the known world reserves.

Large volumes of ore must be mined to produce a small quantity of gold. On the average three tons are needed to produce enough gold for one Krugerrand, the one ounce standard gold coin known all over the world. There are huge mounds of waste materials around Johannesburg, a reminder of the scale of the industry. Now, with new technologies available, these mounds are valuable again as they contain enough gold to warrant reprocessing.

More than a third of the world's gem diamonds are mined in South Africa. These are the large, bright stones so prized for jewellery. However, most diamonds are small and dark, valuable for industrial uses. Their extreme hardness makes them valuable for rock drills and grinding tools. Together, these two types of diamonds provide a high-value export commodity.

There are also other valuable minerals. The iron and steel industry, which fuels a wide range of other manufactures, is based on local deposits of coal and iron ore. All of South Africa's vast mineral wealth is a consequence of the great variety of ancient and more recent rock formations that are found within its borders. The following table of the country's percentages of world reserves for thirteen important minerals illustrates the extent of these resources:

Manganese	93	Alumino-		Zirconium	19
Platinum	83	Silicates	49	Coal	18
Gold	63	Fluorspar	46	Antimony	17
Vanadium	61	Vermiculite	29	Uranium	16
Chrome	58	Diamonds	29		

South African industry is generally concentrated on the high land region around Johannesburg, a city 5,000 feet above sea level; known as the highveld, this area includes most of Orange Free State and extends northward as far as Pretoria and eastward to the Swaziland border. In this region lives more than a third of the nation's people. The jobs in the mines, offices, and factories, are the reasons for the high population density.

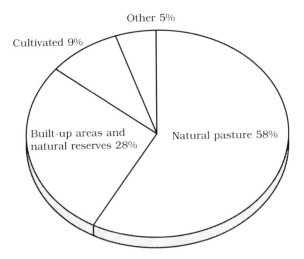

Land use

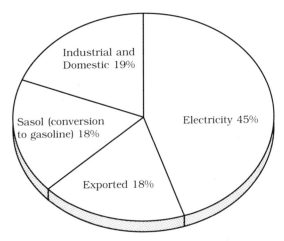

Energy use

The Pretoria-Witwatersrand-Vereeniging (PWV) complex is the heart of the highveld. Its factories produce most of South Africa's manufactured goods, a function of its proximity to the factors of production: minerals, including coal, agricultural products from the nearby farms, water from the Vaal

River, a good transportation network, large local markets, and a skilled labor force.

Recognized trade unions for Blacks in South Africa are less than ten years old. For most of the country's industrial history, registered trade unions were for Whites, Coloreds and Indians only. Surprisingly, it was the left-wing political faction, the Labor Party, which most strongly supported this color bar in order to ensure jobs for the Whites.

In the depression years following World War I, mine-owners proposed bringing in Blacks from neighboring countries, from the colonial territories of Rhodesia as they were known at that time. Wage-cuts for Whites, and lower rates for the additional Black workers, were all part of a plan to reduce costs, in the face of a world economic slump.

The response of the workers was the massive strike of 1922 which turned into a large-scale riot. This tragic episode has become known as the Rand Revolt. More than one hundred died in the ensuing violence. Communist opportunists joined in with what now must be regarded as a strange refrain: "Workers of the world unite for a White South Africa."

In 1979, Blacks finally got the status they needed to look after their interests in negotiations with employers. The Wiehahn Commission recommended that the unions which had been organized by Blacks over the years be given legal status. It also recommended two other vital changes: the abolition of the job reservation clauses, the regulations that prevented Blacks from getting employment in certain work categories, and the inclusion of all workers without discrimination in technical training facilities. The government accepted the Commission's report. The color bar in unions and job opportunities was at last removed.

Traditional thinking does not change quite as quickly as the law. Hundred-year-old attitudes do not disappear overnight. In one supermarket, with branches all over the country, the change has now been made. Promotions are based on merit only. Blacks, Coloreds, Indians and Whites are found at all levels of the company's operations. However, in the five years it took to effect these changes, there was an uphill fight all the way with customers and with management. It will be many years more before Blacks, Coloreds and Indians enjoy to the full the benefits that have already been secured for them by the abolition of discriminatory laws.

In 1886, when the Rand wealth of South Africa was first

discovered, gold had immediate and lasting value as the world's most reliable and most valuable currency. Since that time, this precious metal has lost its status as the real currency behind paper money, yet attitudes have not changed. In fact, in times of financial crisis, gold is prized more than ever, as was seen in its meteoric rise in value following the Arab Oil Crisis of 1973.

Paradoxically, while gold has been dropping on world markets to less than half the price it commanded in the 1970s, South Africa, because of the lower value of the Rand, has maintained the former value of the precious metal. As a result, gold, still the mainstay of South Africa's trade, is pushing the country to new peaks of prosperity, in sharp contrast to the depressed state of Western economies. It is interesting to speculate on what might happen in the future if South Africa, under the pressure of sanctions, retaliated by withholding its gold from the world markets in the midst of an international economic crisis.

Youth violence near Nyanga, Cape Town

10 Boer War III?

Communism is the corruption of a dream of justice.

Adlai Stevenson
Speech at Urbana, 1951

Imagine your morning newspaper with this headline: "Soviet troops invade South Africa: cry of help from Blacks brings quick response." There is no need to develop the background of cause and effect, or note the fact that large numbers of Soviet troops happened to be stationed near at hand when the cry came. The more important fact to observe is the likelihood of the Western world's acceptance of, even indifference to, the invasion, as was the case when Boer War II broke out in 1899. Mutual suspicion and misunderstanding over a long period of time had created a climate of impending crisis. The outbreak of hostilities appeared as an inevitable and even desirable outcome. Britain, the aggressor, was seen as the knight in shining armor, fighting for all that was noble and right, enthusiastically supported by troop contingents from Australia, Canada and New Zealand.

The similarities between the present situation and the period before the 1899 war are startling. Britain, at that time, was the world's greatest imperial power, just as the Soviet Union is today. Her imperialism was backed by an ideology, the notion of the superiority of British administration. Similarly, there is today the conviction in Moscow that its particular form of government is best for the world. The third similarity is the Soviet Union's intense current interest in South Africa, like Britain's in the last quarter of the nineteenth century.

The British methods of conquest in the 1800s were very

much like those of today. First came external pressure; the two independent voortrekker republics were encircled, limiting their contact with other countries. The occupation of Bechuanaland, now Botswana, in 1885, and Zululand in 1887, coupled with a subsequent drive into what is now Zimbabwe, effectively completed the circle of control.

The concerns which led to encirclement stemmed from several unexpected developments following the 1880 Boer War I, when the British were defeated. At the Pretoria Conference which followed, the Transvaal and Orange Free State were given a large measure of freedom. Britain seemed satisfied that the voortrekker republics posed no threat to its empire. It was to be a short-lived period of easy coexistence. Within a few years, the Transvaal government began to build a railway to Delagoa Bay in Portuguese territory, effectively removing its dependence on the railway lines to Durban and Cape Town. In 1886 came the discovery of massive gold deposits on the Rand. Parallelling these events was the acquisition of South West Africa, by Germany, Britain's powerful rival. The Transvaal, especially with the possibility of an Afrikaner-German alliance, had become a serious threat to Britain's expanding empire.

In response to the new situation, Britain, as has already been described in chapter five, launched a series of attacks on the voortrekker republics: stirring discontent among the prospectors and miners because they had no political rights; spreading false information about the Transvaal's neglect of human rights; instigating a revolution; and, finally, forcing open warfare, supported by large-scale contingents of soldiers from Britain's other colonies.

The parallels between these five stages of Britain's conquest, and the events of today, are remarkably similar; even the fifth step, the one suggested by the hypothetical morning newspaper headline, is almost a reality. More than 40,000 soldiers from colonies of the Soviet Union are stationed in Angola, a few miles from the Namibian border.

The present encirclement of South Africa has been going on for some time, to the point where now there is worldwide opposition to all things South African. Scores of countries refuse overflight permission for its airlines, its people are not allowed to participate in international events, its products are banished from store shelves in dozens of countries, and the clamor for sanctions is heard everywhere. It is an encirclement that conveniently serves the interests of the Soviet Union, even though the instigators are often misguided agencies from the Western democracies. The ultimate goal is the same as was Britain's: the weakening of the victim's economic power.

Instead of the *uitlanders*, there are today the Blacks. These people, it is said, because they are disenfranchised, are clamoring for their political rights. It is also widely reported in the Western press that the Blacks are being tortured, and arbitrarily killed, as part of a government policy to control dissent. This is the kind of disinformation to which allusion has already been made in the opening chapter. The reality of the situation is that all recent surveys of Black opinion present a very different picture; for example, surveys continue to show that political rights are far from being the highest priority for most of South Africa's Blacks.

The disinformation campaign does not end there. Like Britain before Boer War II, it is necessary for the Soviet Union to create in the world's eye an image of a noble invader. The ideology of communism, with its universal appeal to the aspirations of humanity, provides such an image. Furthermore, the sheer magnitude of the lies that accompany the ideology will sometimes make them more plausible.

Consider the enormous contradictions in Soviet actions compared with their promises: people are enslaved so they can be free; authoritarian rule is established to secure equality; terrorism becomes the way to security; guerrilla warfare is supposed to bring peace. Seventy years after the revolution that was to bring freedom, equality, and prosperity, none of these things is yet being enjoyed by the people of the Soviet Union; instead, there is a dictatorship at home and an imperial power worldwide, both with minimum interest in the welfare of the peoples they claim to serve.

The Soviet Union is the only imperial power in the field at the present time. The opprobrium associated with imperialism, especially in Africa, has effectively shut out all who might be tempted to compete for modern-day colonies. This is an advantage for the aggressor because it affords time to conquer the region slowly.

No major barrier, other than the military power of the Republic of South Africa, prevents an inexorable Soviet advance. Most of the states of the region are already surrogates. Furthermore, the Soviets have perfected the art of colonial control. Moscow's experience in ruling a multi-racial society at home provided valuable lessons for her African adventures. Strict control, together with adherence to a rigid set of rules, have proved to be very successful formulas for maintaining the stability of an empire.

In pursuance of the disinformation campaign, there is the double-talk by the Communist-led African National Congress (ANC): to Western media, the Freedom Charter, a plea for the peaceful establishment of a democratic country in which all races can participate; to the cells within South Africa, a call for revolutionary violence. Recently a leading member of the ANC summarized the strategy thus: "Make

Buildings torched during a township riot

the death of a collaborator so grotesque that people will never think of doing it."

The Jameson Raid equivalents in present day communist tactics are grotesque indeed. They are focussed in the necklace rituals, a practice that makes the medieval methods of torture and public execution almost humane. Anyone who represents the establishment, a policeman or a municipal official for example, or anyone who is disposed to cooperate with the existing order, is a potential target for the necklace. The practice is approved by well-known Black leaders, and this adds to the difficulty of stamping it out.

The hands are tied behind the victim's back while an automobile tire is put around the neck and set alight. While the murderers dance around the scene, the person dies a slow and agonizing death. In some years there has been a national average of one necklace per day by Black mobs.

The drive for power includes more than murdering local officials. With the Cuban revolution as the model, the ANC and its agents within South Africa decided, in 1984, that the time was ripe for a full-scale peoples' revolt. Boycotts of stores and places of work were initiated, with a view to crippling the economy. Mobs roamed the streets, arbitrarily selecting targets for destruction. Those refusing to go along with particular plans had their homes burned down or were otherwise victimized. Small groups were able to terrorize whole communities in ways such as these.

For a time, the government took no action, since it had often been accused of unwanted interference in township life. Young radicals interpreted this delay as weakness, and assumed that power was shifting into their hands. They intensified their acts of mayhem, persuading others in the process that the revolution was succeeding. When police and military forces finally acted to establish order, it took some time to convince the communist 'comrades' that their perception of power was grievously distorted. The record of violent actions, before and after government intervention, illustrate the high, if misguided, expectations of success that were held by the revolutionaries.

The background to the spiral of unrest which began in 1984 is found in the long-standing policy of the ANC to make the country ungovernable. In the aftermath of a total breakdown in the normal institutions of society, the ANC believes it is the only organization that can take control. If power could be attained, the ANC would be able to silence all dissent by the same dictatorial techniques employed in Mozambique, Angola, and Zimbabwe. The special phase of unrest in 1984 was triggered by the new constitution involving a tricameral parliament. Blacks felt, rightly or wrongly, that they were being finally excluded from participation in the central government. The ANC, in a series of inflammatory pronouncements, sought to capitalize on the discontent, seeking to convince Blacks that their only hope for participation in government lay in violent revolution.

By 1986, violence escalated alarmingly. Within the first five months of that year, 3,500 Black homes, 17,000 cars or buses, and 1,200 schools were destroyed; further, 600 Blacks were killed, half of them by the barbaric necklace method. In the process, there was widespread intimidation and boycotts of schools and other institutions. The plan of the ANC revolutionaries was for the mayhem and fear to climax on 16 June, the tenth anniversary of the 1976 educational crisis; many Sowetan students were killed on that day while protesting Afrikaans as the medium of instruction. The revolutionaries hoped that the strong memories of that tragic day in 1976 would complete the cycle of chaos they had set in motion.

Other organizations, such as the United Democratic Front (UDF), and Azanian Peoples Organization (AZAPO), which were in sympathy with the aims of the ANC and had the freedom to operate within South Africa, planned a one-week series of public protests; their strategy included marches into White areas by Blacks, student boycotts, and large-scale intimidation of those who were not supportive of the protests. With these prospects before him, the State President decided to declare a national State of Emergency effective 12 June, 1986.

The legal basis for this action is enshrined in the South African constitution just as it is in those of other nations. In essence, this provision of law says that if actions by any group of persons threatens either the safety of the public or the maintenance of public order, the government may put aside ordinary laws and substitute emergency regulations. The powers of the government are limited under these circumstances; while there may be summary arrest and detention, parliament must always be informed of the actions taken. Disclosures of this kind allow opposition members to

End of a necklace murder

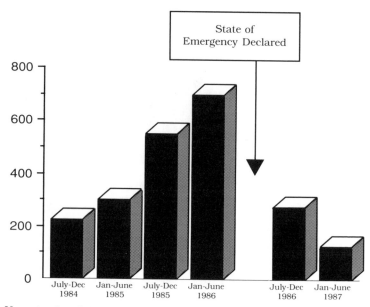

Unrest-related deaths

investigate and, if need be, expose excessive use of the new powers. As the head of a properly constituted, internationally-recognized government, despite the inadequacy of its form of democracy, the State President has every legal right to invoke emergency powers. In the case of the 1986 action, the effects were dramatic: a rapid decline in deaths throughout all the Black communities, restored business confidence and an economic surge over the succeeding two years.

In the aftermath of the crisis, the morale of ANC leaders, as reported by independent observers, has reached its lowest ebb.[43] The total failure of their biggest effort has finally convinced them that they will never succeed militarily. South Africa is not like the many third world states where traditional communist revolutionary techniques have worked. It was no surprise, therefore, to hear, in 1988, of private ANC overtures for talks with the South African government. That strategy might pose a greater threat to government security than would the more overt violence.

The West has often failed to appreciate the continuum, in communist thinking, of military action and diplomacy. All that matters is the final outcome. The end justifies any action, even when the means employed are despicable; if, in a given situation, force does not work, the communist revolutionary will turn negotiator. The object of the exercise is to gain public support by creating an impasse, and using it as proof that the other side refuses to compromise. This is the mode now being employed in South Africa. It explains the absence of serious conflict in the townships throughout the year 1988, the rejection of necklacing by ANC leaders, and the global media campaign to persuade the South African government to come to the ANC negotiating table.

There are good reasons for the Soviet Union's interest in South Africa. In almost all other areas of the continent, it has acquired nothing but liabilities. South Africa could add more wealth to the Soviet Union than the sum of all the African territories it has conquered to date. However, an apparently impregnable military force within South Africa stubbornly resists Soviet advances. Communist leaders have had to recognize, perhaps for the first time in Africa, the inadequacy of their well-worn, brutal techniques of revolutionary violence.

Education is now frequently multi-racial

11 | School: Path to Freedom

Example is the school of mankind, and they will learn at no other.

Edmund Burke

Recent surveys of priorities among Blacks place education as second to everything else. Jobs come first, and equal rights third. The second place standing is a direct result of two developments: the abolition of job reservations and the provision of equal pay for equal work in many of the biggest industries. Education thus becomes the key to advancement, social mobility, and a better standard of living.

The history of White education in South Africa is generally of less interest, because it followed familiar European patterns, and was in place long before the present century. Black education is quite a different story; it remained dependent on missionary societies until 1954, a dependence which provided excellent quality but was severely limited in quantity. When education was taken over by the government, the enormity of the need was faced for the first time. Since then, debate has raged, almost exclusively, around the quality of the government's educational provisions for Blacks.

Like religion, pre-missionary education was closely tied to the social order and was largely informal, with knowledge being acquired from peers through observation. Some formal education did occur during traditional ceremonies and rituals. As Black education assumed the characteristics of modern, Western-style learning, some of the tribal traditions handicapped students. The sense of equality was one element that caused difficulty. As students encountered the

Classrooms are not designed for younger students

competitive aspect of university life, with its emphasis on individual excellence, there was a preference for group performance, in which everyone got a bare pass, and no one excelled.

As early as 1976, President Sebe of Ciskei identified one of the central problems of Black education: the widening gap between school systems and their human environments. In his view, when people first receive an education, a desire for more is created. He illustrates his argument from the case of an illiterate parent whose child learns to read. There is an immediate demand for access to higher levels of learning. Later, when that child grows up and has children, the new parents want better education for their children than they had. Alongside this spiral of improving educational standards is the high birth and comparatively low death rates, which add to the numbers of uneducated people at the lower end of the scale.

What has been the response of the central government? Financially, there has been a steady increase in the proportion of the national budget allocated to Black education. In spite of this, the government has been perceived as offering an inferior service to Blacks while providing superior opportunities for Whites.

This perception of inequity was predictable, since there had been a history of 'special' education for Blacks, derogatorily dubbed 'Bantu Education', and because efforts at improvement seemed to be meeting with limited success. Another reason for negative attitudes was language usage. Students were often compelled to study subjects in Afrikaans instead of being allowing a choice in regard to the medium of instruction. A similar problem is often found in Canada, when English-speaking sectors of the country are forced to make provision for French in the various institutions of society. The Soweto riots of 1976 were, in large part, a protest against the language problem.

One of the most common criticisms from other countries is the per capita differential between money for White education and that for Black. All South African teachers, independently of their color, receive the same salary after their teacher training courses are completed; since 80 percent of school budgets goes into salaries, the expenditure differences, as between White and Black school systems, are mainly due to the delays in getting Black teachers up to the standards of Whites. At present, about half of all Black teachers, 60,000 in all, have not yet graduated from high school.

In assessing the amounts of money spent on education, frequently the massive contributions from the private sector are overlooked. For many years, British, Canadian, and U.S. institutions, both private and public, have been assisting in the upgrading of Black education. In order to avoid the appearance of cooperating with an apartheid system, their efforts are channelled through private agencies. Independent universities are one expression of this aid. Inservice training centres are another. South African teachers are given a year's sabbatical leave on full salary every five years. The incentive to upgrade educational levels, and thus get a better salary, leads large numbers of these teachers to spend their sabbatical year at one of the public or private inservice training centres.

Within South Africa, the business community is actively involved in private education. One building company, in 1987, spent more than US$3 million on special private schools for intellectually-gifted Blacks. Multi-racial, residential secondary schools are in operation in many parts of the country, providing high quality education in the context of a community that is free from all traces of apartheid. For less fortunate students who have had inadequate preparation at school, but who are intellectually capable of obtaining a university degree, there are special university one-year preparation courses, again funded by local or foreign aid agencies. At the University of Witwatersrand, in Johannesburg, in any given year, there are more than one hundred students taking this kind of special one-year course.

In the rural areas, where more than half of the Black population still lives, farmers take responsibility for erecting school buildings and making them ready for use. The government then provides teachers for the schools. These arrangements only apply to the White areas of the country. Within the Black rural villages, the situation is not so good, except where there is private funding. The government money meets only part of the educational costs. The balance is met by the members of the community, yet another example of private input and an indication of the high priority accorded education, even by very poor people.

Overall, the government has made significant gains, despite enormous obstacles. The total number of Blacks in school jumped 35 percent from 4.8 million in 1980 to 6.5 in 1988. More importantly, this increase alone required the construction of three new schools every school day, every year, just to maintain standards and provide space for the extra students.

The government stepped up its financial contribution to Black education by 600 percent, from US$200 million in 1980, to US$1200 million in 1988. The growth in money for White education in the same period was negligible. The extra expenditure brought good results: the number of students gaining university entrance rose sharply, the average teacher to pupil ratio rose to 1:39, and the percentage of Blacks attending secondary schools jumped from 16 to 21 percent, one of the highest rates in all of Africa.

In 1981 the De Lange Commission handed down its extensive report on education. The criticisms were severe and carried the strong recommendation that adequate progress could only be made if all groups were brought under a single ministry of education. In 1984 the government accepted this recommendation for a single office at the national level, established a new ministry, and granted it four-fold power: determining all financial allocations, setting salary levels and conditions of employment, organizing the professional registration of teachers, and standardizing all examinations.[12]

The new act that followed the policy decision states in unequivocal terms that every person living in the Republic of South Africa, regardless of color, sex, or religion, is entitled to the same educational opportunity. An executive, comprising the heads of what had formerly been separate administrations, meets regularly to administer the new Department of National Education.

In order to assist the Minister of Education and his executive in carrying out their mandate, several committees have been struck, all of them multi-racial in composition: the South African Council for Education (SACE) advises the minister on educational matters generally, including in-school and out-of-school programs, plus pre-service and in-service training of teachers; two committees on educational structures deal with salaries, promotions, registration and certification.

While it might seem, at first glance, that all of this is a total

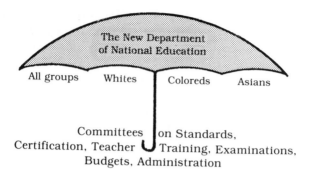

The New Department of National Education

departure from former practice, in fact many of the things in the new act have been policy for some time. For several years, teachers with the same qualifications have been paid identical salaries while all examinations have been based on a single core syllabus and controlled by one authority.

The gains that have been made must be evaluated in the light of an expanding school population which, in turn, is the result of rising standards of living plus increasing demands by industry for a highly educated work force. The increases first occur at the lowest rung of the educational ladder, while the upper school years maintain their traditional pattern of drop-outs. It is common practice for a member in a large family to attend school for four or five years, then go to work for several years while another member of the family gets a chance to attend school. Because of this habit, it is not unusual to see a 25-year-old in an elementary school classroom.

Because of the demands from industry for higher and higher educational standards, the length of time spent in school is steadily increasing. Over the past decade the number of students completing high school has multiplied tenfold from five thousand to fifty thousand.

Alongside the burgeoning day-school population, there is a massive adult education program. The number of people involved is more than twice the total regular school population. When not at work, these adults attend special classes, many of them funded and hosted by their employers, as one more example of privately-funded education.

Greatly increased government funding can and has made

rapid progress in the provision of physical facilities and teaching materials. However, training of teachers and coping with cultural barriers are not so easily accelerated. Psychological factors, such as large families or poor self-image among under-privileged families, interfere with school attendance.

The decision to unite all educational institutions under a single umbrella was a momentous step, marking the end of a long-standing policy of several different kinds of educational provisions, based on a system of racial segregation. Because of the high value placed on education in today's technological society, this development was a particularly strong rejection of traditional apartheid policy.

Residents of Alexandra Township protest rents of new homes

12 | Media Myopia

It is not the magnitude of the terrorist operation that counts but the publicity.

Michael Hough
Terrorism and Publicity

The second half of the twentieth century has witnessed an explosion of communication media: newspapers, magazines, satellites, computers, television. By far the most influential of these is television. It has changed the way we see things, and it has threatened our values. When, day after day, this visual medium presents us with accounts of war, sadism, discrimination, natural disasters, accidental deaths, even malicious crimes, each sandwiched between comedy and hilarious advertisements, tragedy becomes entertainment; instead of a natural revulsion on our part, there is passive acceptance.

Every journalist knows that stories about power, crime, sex, money, tragedy, and racism are the things that sell newspapers and interest television watchers; selling papers, or increasing viewing audiences is, of course, first priority for publisher and broadcaster alike. By definition, news deals with the extraordinary; hence ordinary events, or average conditions, appear less frequently in the mass media. As a result, we are given a skewed image of the world, a record of occasional, often bizarre events that will pique our interest long enough for the advertiser to make his pitch.

These distorted pictures of life are harmless when they come from local or familiar places. Experiences and other sources of information provide a balance. It is a very different story when the report comes from lesser-known regions. Caricatures of people and countries become standard fare. In an earlier generation, when print was the principal source

Victim of street violence

of information, libraries provided balance, offsetting the limitations of the newspaper.

It is much more difficult to compensate for television bias; for most people, seeing is believing. There is no felt need for additional information. The facts that the thirty-second clip is only a partial image of an event, that audience interest dominates item selection, and that the personal philosophy of the network anchorperson also affects choices, are largely lost on the viewer. The immediacy, color, action, and fascination of the story carry their own intrinsic authenticity.

Surveys of television network anchorpersons reveal remarkable similarities in personal values and interests. Research reports on the characteristics of North America's media elite list these values as dominant: sympathy for socialist philosophies and dislike of capitalism; intolerance of views contrary to their own; and rejection of traditional American religious and family values. The existence of similar biases in the news sources most used by these media elite confirmed the research findings.[44]

Recently, a research report from the Hoover Institute at Stanford University revealed the pro-communist leanings of many members of the Canadian Broadcasting Corporation (CBC). Arnold Beichman, author of the report, cites a CBC television documentary on the African National Congress (ANC) in which communist influences in the organization are barely mentioned. Beichman points out that the ANC is one of the most Soviet-penetrated political organizations in all of Africa. To overlook the political leanings of the ANC avoids a central issue of its motivation.

Beichman's report goes on to list the many facets of the ANC's ties with communism. The organization receives financial support from the Soviet Union, and half of its executive is shared with the South African Communist Party. Further, the ANC has made common cause with the goals of the Soviet Union at numerous conferences. Beichman depicts the CBC's documentary of the ANC as lying by omission. Like so many others in the North American media, according to Beichman, CBC reporters and anchorpersons contend they are not communists, but the evidence makes it plain that they share a similar perspective.

Beichman's critique does not end with an assessment of one telecast. The CBC is described as having been a disgrace to honest journalism for years. Beichman cites the network's treatment of Central American guerrillas and of Fidel Castro as indicative of its bias. In conclusion, Beichman makes it clear that he does not support the South African government. He has severely criticized it ever since he first wrote about apartheid in 1965. His plea is simply a call for more objectivity or, at least, a shift from the constant coverage of only one side of issues and events.

The personal philosophies of media people are important today. It was not always so. A generation ago, every effort was made to hide the opinions, even the name, of the messenger who bore the news. Objectivity was all important. Now, this outlook has given way to idolizing the million-dollar anchor-person, to the point where personal opinion is almost synonymous with fact. These changes drew the following statement from Ted Koppel, the famous ABC television anchorman, "It is easy to be seduced into believing that what we are doing is just fine. After all, we get money, fame, and even influence. But money, fame and influence, without responsibility, are the assets of a courtesan."

Public confidence in the media has been declining in recent years. Since the mid-1970s, percentage acceptance of the reliability of television information has dropped from 30 percent to 25 percent, and newspapers from 25 percent to 20 percent. Surprisingly, confidence in statements from the military has risen in the same period.[45] Part of the explanation lies in the enormous power and wealth of the media elite. People react negatively to this sort of thing, just as they do to big labor, big business, and big government.

The U.S. discovered the destructive power of biassed television during the Vietnam War. Cameras from the main networks had easy access to the allied war zone. They shot scenes of soldiers getting killed, of bases being lost, and of combat action in which civilians were sometimes slaughtered. The only footage they were able to get from the other side was carefully doctored to show courageous action, success in battle, and humanitarian treatment of civilians and captured soldiers. The striking contrasts were piped into U.S. living rooms night after night. It was not long before the war that was being won in Asia was disastrously lost at home. America surrendered. When U.S. forces landed on Grenada, some years later, television networks were told politely to stay at home.

South Africa entered the television age much later than Europe and North America. It took the country some time to learn what the U.S. had so painfully discovered in Vietnam, and the lesson was a costly one. ANC terrorists carefully staged protests before the cameras, often ensuring that a child would get into both the line of fire and the cameras at the same time. At one point, while television was still being given full rein, deaths ran at a rate of two a day. When the government barred the cameras, the number suddenly dropped to about one a week.

There is a problem in giving freedom to the media and

then removing it. The television moguls are upset. They have lost first rate footage, and they become enemies, always looking for some excuse to paint a negative picture of the territory they lost. How much easier it is for the Soviet Union. They know what to do, and they do not have to worry about the niceties of public opinion.

Early in 1988, serious unrest broke out in Armenia, a province of the Soviet Union. Many were killed. Eveyone knew that Western cameras would not be allowed into the area, because the Soviet Union has a long history of successfully hiding distasteful events. It was no surprise, therefore, when the Moscow correspondent of the Canadian Broadcasting Corporation (CBC) reported that the country is very sensitive about the violence and deaths in Armenia, especially because it is caused by ethnic conflict. He added that the Soviet Union doesn't want to parade its problems on TV.

The CBC is one of North America's worst examples of biassed television journalism. For years it has favored communist movements in Central America and Africa, sympathizing with their difficulties, and heaping scorn on Western resistance to their advances. It has interviewed terrorists who represent a small minority of Blacks, yet are trying to destroy the South African economy, while, at the same time, refusing to meet with legitimate representatives of the Black majority in that country.

Of all the agencies that use television for wrong purposes, terrorist organizations are the most skilled and most successful. Ted Koppel describes their work in this way: "Television and terrorists have a symbiotic relationship. Without television, international terrorism is powerless." Western societies, or perhaps Western journalists, assume, falsely, that extreme actions like terrorism, must have obvious causes in the social environment of the people concerned. This is precisely the conclusion the terrorist wants the media to draw. Free air-time worldwide is provided, and the media people, having convinced themselves that they are serving a worthwhile cause, find that their viewers are riveted to the screens. It is good business.

George Will, a U.S. columnist, describes the telecasting of terrorist scenes as a failure of intelligence and an abrogation of moral reponsibility. "The direct causes of terrorism are terrorists", says Will, "and the indirect causes are regimes that support or tolerate them." He goes on to point out that terrorists are far from being desperate men. Many are children of privilege. Often the act of terrorism is a game, a potent instrument of self-expression.[46]

Both print and video media have treated South Africa as a pariah state, about which little or no good thing can be said. Daily the country is described as "the white-minority government of South Africa". This adjectival phrase has come to be the standard label used in reference to the country. It is little wonder that the South African government, in an attempt to correct the imbalance, will not allow foreign reporters to use phrases like "minority-white regime", or "riot-torn South Africa", in despatches to overseas papers. Imagine the consternation in Africa if other countries carried labels like South Africa's: "the tribal dictatorship of Zimbabwe", or "the minority dictatorship of Burundi".

The fascination with South Africa is as ubiquitous as the media distortions about the country. In one recent three-month period, the *New York Times* and the *Washington Post*, together, carried 415 stories about South Africa. These stories, even trivial ones like a school boycott, were frequently given front page treatment, while massacres of 50 or more people in India, on the same day, were typically given an insignificant amount of space on the back cover. During the three-month period in question, the total number of stories on the rest of Africa, by the two papers, only amounted to seventy-five.[47]

The content of the daily horror stories from South Africa gives an impression of a terrible place in which to live, since the news coverage focuses on violence, death, destruction, and the suppression of information about anti-government activity. No one would suspect that the real reason for so many South African stories coming to North America is that many of the correspondents who are assigned to Africa decide to live in South Africa, the most livable part of the continent. To justify their presence there, they have to send daily reports of what they claim to be important events.

As South Africa tackles the abuse of media privileges by Western correspondents, it is accused of muzzling the press and withholding information, just as the Soviet Union and similar dictatorships are wont to do; yet the editor of one of South Africa's biggest dailies, the Johannesburg *Star*, thinks otherwise. James Clarke asserts that no important information, only opinion, is being withheld from the rest of the world. Nevertheless, the image of extreme censorship persists, bolstered by those who sustain the delusion by using old footage or the occasional video smuggled out of the country. The mass media wields enormous power to inform in today's society. However, since its effectiveness derives from style rather than accuracy, it is also potentially misleading. Because the distinction between these two qualities is frequently blurred, an understanding of South Africa hinges on the ability to assess media reliability.

Part Three

A New Nation

*We are determined to proceed
with our reform programme
which has already reached an
advanced stage, whatever the
obstacles we have to contend
with; and we want to get moving
with the negotiations, for this is
the key to the solution of our
problems. Our political programme provides for power sharing, subject only to the protection
of the rights of all minorities,
and we are reconciled to the
eventual disappearance of
white domination.*

From a letter written by the South
African State President, P. W. Botha,
to the Commonwealth Eminent
Persons Group on Southern Africa,
December, 1985.

Protest leader carrying communist flag

13 | Protest Politics

Give every man thy ear but few thy voice.

William Shakespeare
Hamlet

It is quite impossible for South Africa to model its future constitution on what has been achieved elsewhere. There is no nation or community, anywhere, that has been faced with a comparable situation. Some efforts have been made to find a similar history in other countries. The inclusion of Japan in these quests is interesting; in that land, a minority had ruled for centuries, then was overthrown in 1868 in a bloodless transfer of power. The former elite remained part of the new order. The main cause of change was rapid economic growth coupled with increasing ties throughout the world, a condition corresponding to South Africa in the 1970s.

Because of the difficulty of finding political parallels, there is a plethora of theories, and a host of advocates, inside and outside South Africa, who claim to know what should be done. South Africa has, in fact, become a favorite laboratory for political theorists. The responsibility of those in power is to weigh the ideas presented, and take the best actions it can, in the on-going search for representative government.

It is easy to dismiss the violent options presented by such organizations as the African National Congress (ANC), the Pan-Africanist Congress (PAC), and the South African Communist Party (SACP). These three organizations offer simplistic solutions to complex social problems, together with the conviction, albeit an increasingly weak one, that they can implement their programs militarily. As banned organizations, they have been been forced to operate outside the country, with diminishing support from those within South Africa.

By far the largest number of political theorists are the non-violent protest groups. They operate within the country, some via bona fide parliamentary opposition parties, others, disillusioned with existing political channels, through new extra-parliamentary organizations. From these groups the government regularly receives lists of its failures along with proposals for alternative policies. In many instances these protest groups represent a preliminary stage of development, a sorting out of options, in the long process of resolving the nation's political destiny.

For more than thirty years, the Progressive Federal Party (PFP) has served as opposition in Parliament. It maintained the best traditions of the Westminster model of government, with widespread acceptance and support from all of South Africa's ethnic groups. Early in the 1980s, after many years as PFP leader, Frederik van Zyl Slabbert concluded that parliamentary opposition was useless; he left to form the Institute for a Democratic Alternative for South Africa (IDASA), outside of Parliament, hoping thereby to secure greater co-operation with Blacks.

Slabbert's move was followed by two others: Denis Worrall, former South African Ambassador to Britain, left to form the Independent Party (IP); and Wynand Malan set up yet another organization, the National Democratic Movement (NDM). The differences among these three new splinter groups are small; whether or not to recognize ethnic groups as political entities is the biggest difference between IP and NDM. All three parties have been well received throughout the country. However, the critical element of electoral support has not yet been evident; the votes went to the right of centre at the last election, not the left.

All the indicators of the past three years point to a concern among Whites over the mode of transition to Black enfranchisement. Their fears are by no means expressions of color prejudice. There is worry over the effects on the economy, and safety in the mines, just to mention two areas of concern. The manifestos of all three groups lack policy statements on how the transition process would be handled.

Robin Friedland of the *Financial Mail* thinks a qualified franchise should have been included as an interim step. He suggests, for starters, an arrangement based on income level, property ownership, and educational achievement. "This", he says, "ought to be accompanied by an economic plan that would secure these standards for most Blacks within a generation." Friedland adds that a graduated move of this kind would prevent the sudden emergence of a destructively radical electorate.[48]

IDASA, NDM, and IP, while multi-racial, are closely related to the White community, and have many links to those within Parliament. The United Democratic Front (UDF), yet another protest group, is quite a different organization. It was launched in 1983, within the non-White community, under the leadership of Dr. Allan Boesak, in order to challenge the

Reverend Allan Boesak

government on the exclusion of Blacks from the new Tricameral Parliament. The UDF soon served as an umbrella for all kinds of opposition groups. Many of its members overstepped the limits of peaceful protest and were incarcerated; by 1985, it was serving as surrogate for the banned ANC.

While maintaining a non-violent stance, in order to avoid being banned, UDF members rarely condemned the terrorist incursions from neighboring countries and, in fact, sympathized with all those who chose to protest violently. Early in 1987, murderous rivalry broke out in townships around Pietermaritzburg, Natal, between UDF members and Zulu organizations. The area is part of the KwaZulu self-governing homeland; because of their refusal to support violence, the Zulus saw the killings as revenge by ANC adherents. Within a two-month period, 200 people lost their lives before the homeland authorities brought things under control.

Intimidation of those who do not support their policies is one of the UDF techniques. Pamphlets are issued to homes by the comrades, as the young revolutionaries are called, demanding specific contributions from each member of a household, and warning that "they will be dealt with in the usual way", to quote from one UDF circular, if money is not forthcoming when the comrades call to collect.

The various problems created by UDF behavior were further aggravated as a result of the involvement of radical churches. People became confused, both locally and worldwide, over the thinking of South Africa's Christians. Throughout history, churches, both Protestant and Catholic, viewed the proclamation of the gospel as their purpose, not the advocacy of solutions to political and social problems. Individuals, as citizens, can and should take up these concerns, but not the church. This traditional position was recently reaffirmed by the Pope and other church leaders.

Because the church is seen, especially among South Africans, as an important, high-profile institution, its views carry more weight than its numbers might suggest. The parallel case in North America is the status accorded Hollywood film stars; because they are so famous, their views are often treated with great respect beyond their due.

The radicals, the so-called South African Council of Churches (SACC), represent a minority of the nation's Christians, less than 25 percent. Furthermore, since it is dominated by the English churches, the SACC reminds

Afrikaners of the hatred and scorn they once endured at the hands of the English. The vast majority of the churches, and the overwhelming majority of the total Christian population, on the basis of New Testament teaching, is loyal to the government in power.

In many ways, SACC's behavior is quite perplexing, if not suspect. Over 90 percent of its funding comes from sources outside South Africa, an extraordinary situation for an institution that claims to represent a country. Its preoccupation with Black liberation is very evident but, unfortunately, it is not matched with a corresponding concern for Blacks; many SACC churches show declining Black membership. Most controversial is its identification with a theological document called *Kairos*, a Greek word meaning moment of truth, which declares that God is on the side of the SACC, and is against the government.[49]

The Kairos Document was drawn up by members of various South African churches who met in Soweto in the summer of 1985. Two months later Dr. Beyers Naude, General Secretary of the SACC, presented it to the World Council of Churches (WCC) in Geneva as a challenge to the church. Subsequently it was translated and republished in many countries. The authors of the original document have chosen to remain anonymous, but the origins of Kairos are clear. They are centred in an international movement known as contextual theology, and this document is a local version of the movement.

Three types of Christians are identified in Kairos. The first consists of all who uphold the present political system. Their position is described as state theology and is soundly condemned. A second group includes those who are totally dissatisfied with the present system and wish to see change. However, their views of change imply reconciliation, justice, and non-violence. They are described by the authors of Kairos as church theology thinkers and condemned as old-fashioned and outdated. The third category of Christian thinking is called prophetic theology. It is based on social analysis and calls for revolutionary change.

The assumption of prophetic theology is that God takes the side of the oppressed. The document therefore goes on to propose a detailed set of instructions to the churches which will direct them into appropriate political action. These directions include a complete transformation of all normal activities including worship, administration of sacraments, and counselling. In essence, prophetic theology, like marxist strategy, proposes that the socio-economic evils of the present system must first be radically exposed and renounced, in order to justify the second step of planned radical change.

At its heart, prophetic theology parts company with the long history of Christian thinking in all branches of the church. In the opinion of the Kairos authors, traditional thinking is abstract, indifferent to the real problems of society, and tends to justify the political status quo. From this perspective, it is a kind of court theology, siding with the established rulers against the best interests of the lower classes of society.

The characteristic technique of Kairos replaces deductive modes by inductive ones. For example, instead of taking the Bible or one of the creeds as the starting point, prophetic theology begins with the given social order and bends theology until it meets social needs. This social analysis precedes even the reading of the Bible, so that the latter is read selectively with texts being accepted or discarded as they do or do not fit the social interests of the reader. This method is quite similar to marxist philosophy, in that the underlying principle of analysis is the class struggle between rich and poor, between the oppressor and the oppressed.

Richard Neuhaus is particularly critical of the Kairos statement because it reminds him of the position taken by some German churches at the time of Hitler. "The partisan church is an apostate church", he says. "No worldly order or would-be order can be equated with the Kingdom of God. The finality of unavoidable revolution, implied by the Kairos document, is a new and more rigorous apartheid than the original it claims to oppose."[50]

In spite of the position taken by a few churches, many people believe that a religious approach is the best solution to inter-group problems, since religion is a common social element. In earlier days, a religious section was found at the back of every village hut where sacrificial offerings were placed on a raised platform. The head of the household was the priest, and his social standing in the community defined his responsibilities. This influence of religion has remained as a formative influence in Black society.

Christian influences date from 1488 when Bartolomeu Dias set up a cross near what is now Port Elizabeth. Since that time, millions have come into association with various branches of Christianity. The largest and fastest growing present-day sector is the African Independent Churches. Because they do not use intoxicants, drugs, or cigarettes, they are able to take care of their families, and assist others who may be in need because of misfortune or unemployment. Since healing constitutes a major part of their regular services, they also take care of the sick.

Most of them have no buildings, so they meet in homes. They provide all the financial and leadership support they need from their own membership. Their numbers are growing at a tremendous rate: from 2,000 denominations and

Bishop Isaac Mokoena, President of the Reformed Independent Black churches, whose membership is over five million

2 million members in 1960, to more than 4,000 and 6 million today. They represent 30 percent of the total South African population.[51] Other branches of Christianity represent proportions as follows: Dutch Reformed Church 14%; Methodists 10%; Roman Catholics 9%; Anglicans 7%; various others, together, 7%. This amounts to a 77 percent Christian South Africa.

Christian denominations are multi-racial, some uniformly so in all of their churches, some with separate buildings and administration for different ethnic groups. Paradoxically, the one denomination that is most frequently accused of supporting apartheid, the Dutch Reformed Church (DRC), was the first to institute a common membership for all racial groups; that occurred in the early days of settlement at the Cape. Slaves were part of the common community and received their freedom after baptism. For many churches, this kind of integrated life ended in 1857, when separate congregations appeared. At the 1986 DRC Conference, the original pattern was reinstated, and the Church again opened its doors to people of all races.

The majority of South Africa's Christians, as has been said, see the proclamation of the gospel as their main work, while a minority of church leaders feel that, for them, protest, confrontation, even sabotage of government plans, are appropriate first priorities. There is a third category, advocated by a still smaller number of people, which represents a unique, yet typically South African approach to protest. It is based on the work of Mahatma Gandhi, who spent many years in Natal, between 1893 and 1915, refining and demonstrating this approach.[52]

Gandhi's term for protest was *satyagraha*, meaning force of truth, and his ideas were, in part, derived from the life of Jesus. In essence, Gandhi proposed a response of love to whatever form of victimization was being experienced. Instead of yielding to, say, intimidation in the townships, the victim refuses to follow instructions, and accepts the ghastly necklace punishment that comes with refusal.

The effect of this kind of behavior, claim its advocates, is to weaken the resolve of those perpetrating crimes, so that they reform. It worked in South Africa during the time of Gandhi. Unjust laws were changed without bloodshed, just because some people were prepared to suffer, without malice, for the stand they took. It worked in India because

Gandhi persuaded vast numbers of people to adopt his approach. More recently, during the terror reign of Idi Amin in Uganda, many Christians employed a form of satyagraha, to blunt the edge of the brutality meted out by Blacks to fellow Blacks.

The protests and violence of the period 1983 to 1987, are not easily forgotten by the White community. People saw the ANC attempting, through its agents in the townships, to overthrow the government. They witnessed the killing of hundreds of Blacks near Pietermaritzburg, all because of political disagreements. The passage of time will undoubtedly help to assuage White fears because, increasingly, the use of violence for political ends is being discredited. By the year 2000, the present pace of reform will have resolved most of the nation's problems. The protest politics of the 1980s will have vanished.

The circling of wagons, or laager, depicted on the walls of the
Voortrekker Monument (above), Pretoria

14 | Partition Option

Great wits are sure to madness near allied,
And thin partitions do their bounds divide.

John Dryden
Absalom and Achitophel, 1680

The spectacular success of the Conservative Party (CP) in the May election of 1987 revived a long-standing constitutional proposal, that of partition. The CP is an offshoot of the governing National Party (NP). It broke away in 1982 over proposals to introduce Indians and Coloreds into Parliament. This action represented the first major crack in the strong, 40-year-old unity of the Afrikaners who took power in 1948. As a result of the 1987 election, the official parliamentary opposition has shifted, for the first time in decades, from the liberal Progressive Federal Party (PFP) to the CP.

The Conservatives, and those who support them, represent the old-line Afrikaner community, the people who enthusiastically approved the new apartheid laws in the 1950s. They have consistently held to the view that South Africa should never become a multi-racial, integrated society. Although their numbers are small, less than 30 percent of the White electorate at most, they exploit outbreaks of township violence by reminding people of past conflicts with Blacks, and advocating the benefits of completely separate communities.

The new concept of partition, while true to the basic design of apartheid, is quite different in application from the ideas of the 1950s. Then, the whole scheme was imposed unilaterally, by the White community, on the various tribal groups and other non-Whites; now, negotiation, and sacrificial sharing of resources on the part of the Whites, are characteristics of the discussions that are taking place. As a result, the partition idea has become popular with both ends of the political spectrum, because it seems, at first glance, to resolve some intractable difficulties.

The CP's future plans envisage an Afrikaner territory extending from the northern Transvaal, through the Orange Free State and the northern portion of the Cape. This area includes the large majority of the Afrikaner population. Once delimited, on the basis of an agreement with the rest of the country, and after acceptance as a member of the United Nations, this Afrikaner community would become an independent nation. It would have its own constitution and laws, and people from 'South Africa' would be welcomed as immigrants.

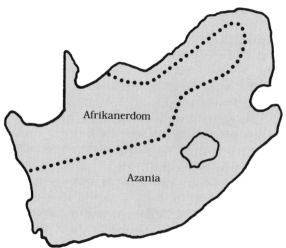

Recent partition proposal

The Conservatives have no policy for the rest of South Africa. They feel it is not their responsibility to prescribe either forms of government or territorial redistribution, although they would expect some sort of economic association with future political structures. They consider the gold, and some other mines, to be part of the Black communities; otherwise, the economic disparities between Afrikanerdom and 'South Africa' would lead to conflict.

Tragically, the twin motives behind partition are not the altruistic ideals promulgated in policy platforms. Like the ostrich, which appears to hide its head in the sand at signs of danger, the Conservatives turn away from the present, when difficulties arise, and go back to discarded ideas from the nineteenth century. Leading members still feel that the Black is inferior, in terms of intellectual calibre, never able to rise to White levels of achievement. That kind of thinking was popular a century ago but has been discarded in modern times.

The second motivating drive is fear. The sense of an impending fight for survival, like the old Zulu wars, pervades Conservative thinking. They see the growing disparities in numbers between Whites and Blacks, along with the National Government's plans for a fully-integrated society, and they have visions of a second Blood River debacle. This time, they wonder who will be the winner. Alan Paton, shortly before his death in 1988, stressed this fundamental weakness in segments of Afrikaner society:

> There is a feeling for Blacks, a compound of fear and hatred. It is not a feeling that is cherished by all Afrikaners, and no doubt the hatred has much abated, but the fear is still there, and if we do not understand that, we do not understand the politics of South Africa.[53]

Had the apartheid dream of Dr. H. F. Verwoerd materialized, in the early 1950s, there would be no need for a CP. Ten independent Black nations, each with its own citizenship, would have ensured the permanence of a White area within South Africa. Fortunately, that dream has faded into oblivion. With the light of hindsight, no one, not even the Conservatives, want to go back to it. The new dream will be a negotiated partition, no matter what costs, or lower standards of living, are demanded from the Whites. However, the Conservatives first hope to gain political power, and rearrange the nation's infrastructure, conforming it to their goals; whether by agreement under existing conditions, or via a majority government, there is a firm determination to establish Afrikanerdom within this century.

Meanwhile, the CP is publicizing its deep roots in the history of South Africa. The year 1988 ideally served for that purpose. It was the 150th anniversary of the famous Great Trek, when the British colonial yoke proved too much for the settlers, and they migrated northward in search of new territory. That quest involved extended conflict with Blacks be-

Statue of King Shaka at Ulundi, the capital of KwaZulu

fore they finally settled in the two interior Afrikaner republics. It was a short-lived freedom. The British moved northward, virtually destroyed the structure of their society in the
grim and unjust Boer War II, then brought Afrikanerdom
under British control once more.

Partition has been a favourite solution to the problems of
divided societies. It has been used many times over the past
forty years. India, at independence, resolved its religious
conflict between Moslems and Hindus by dividing the country into India and Pakistan; subsequently, Pakistan split
into Pakistan and Bangladesh after a bloody civil war. In
Cyprus, dividing the new nation into two parts proved to be
the only solution to resolving tensions between Turks and
Greeks. Minorities in Ireland, India, Sri Lanka, and Ethiopia
continue to struggle to secure partition.

The partition option, as an alternative to Grand Apartheid, has been under some discussion in South Africa for
more than 20 years, but its first strong showing dates from
the mid-1970s. Several events combined, at that time, to
raise serious questions about social conditions: Portuguese
abandonment of Angola and Mozambique; increasing worldwide opposition to the concept of independent homelands;
and the Soweto riots of 1976. Many of the arguments advanced at that time are still being applied today.

Some of the arguments of the mid-1970s stressed the historical claims of Whites. One widely circulated map, prepared by Blacks as a parody of the homelands concept, proposed a 'Whitestan', consisting of an area within 100 km of
Cape Town, matching the size of the Dutch Colony of 1700.
Some proposed adding territory to correspond with the Cape
Colony boundaries as of 1798. Such a Whitestan might well
be defensible historically, as a place for Whites, Coloreds,
and Indians, as it does not impinge on lands taken from
Blacks.[54]

Historical claims, however, are only a part of the argument. The economic development of the nation must also be
considered. On that score, a plan outlined in 1976 proposed
dividing the country along a line stretching from Port Elizabeth to Bloemfontein and Kimberley, and thence to the Botswana border. Such a division would have historical justifica-
tion and, to a substantial degree, provide an economic base
for an independent country.[55]

Whatever partition plan is proposed, there is a risk of un-

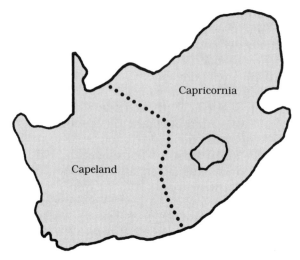

Partition proposal from the mid-1970s

expected inequities surfacing, leaving open the possibility of
a takeover by the bigger member. In the minds of Conservatives, this would be safeguarded by United Nations membership, and because the initial division was a mutual, voluntary agreement. Not everyone sees it that way. African experience has led some to say that broken treaties shower the continent like confetti. Many South African Whites would insist
on a formal military alliance with the West as the only adequate safeguard. Even so, the logistics of military action at
such a distance would pose enormous problems for Western
nations, as Britain discovered during the Falklands War of
1982.

Thus, accompanying any partition, given the living standards of most South Africans, staggering amounts of aid
would be essential, in order to bring the Black half up to the
standards of the Whites. As will be shown in chapter eigh-
teen, this means more than aid for South Africa. There is the
dependent network linking many neighboring states. An extended breakdown of South Africa's transportation, industrial, and social systems would bankrupt half a dozen of
these states. The cost of substitution for South Africa's systems would demand the entire aid resources of the international community.

While the strong showing of the CP in the 1987 election is

the main reason for the recent focus on partition, more recent developments have kept it alive. The pressure of sanctions, while not yet seriously disrupting the economy, has reduced job opportunities and limited wage increases for Whites. The reaction has been a swing to the CP by the working-class, somewhat reminiscent of the 1920s, when a threat to their jobs led to the Rand Revolt. Thus sanctions, far from removing apartheid, entrench it by bolstering those who call for its retention.

A map of White political constituencies illustrates the extent of the trend: new support for the CP follows the coal seams, not the farming areas, the traditional Conservative base. Furthermore, whereas board rooms and reception areas of offices are increasingly scrapping their separate facilites, the factory floors hang on to 'White men' and 'Non-White Men' washrooms. Against this growing strength of conservatism, however, there is the integration of Whites, Indians, and Coloreds in Parliament. The National Party, the reformers, are assured of a clear majority for some time to come.

The most interesting development of all, in this renaissance of partition, is ANC involvement. As a result of their 1985-86 fiasco, when attempts at a violent solution failed, and their popularity plummetted, the ANC is looking at non-violent alternatives. Under a partition plan, the non-Whites would get their own country and the Whites theirs. Once independent, even if major concessions had to be made in the process, the ANC could mount a massive military build-up, with the aid of the Soviet Union; partition, paradoxically, would have promoted not peace but instead the original ANC goal of violent conquest.

Mangosuthu G. Buthelezi, Chief Minister of KwaZulu and
President of Inkatha

15 | Multi-Racial Natal

*All government is founded on compromise and
barter.*

Edmund Burke

The various protest groups described in chapter thirteen represent minority organizations, mostly extra-
parliamentary ones. Partition, the subject of chapter
fourteen, is a serious constitutional proposal from the official opposition in Parliament. The new, multi-racial design,
developed in South Africa's province of Natal, is a third approach to constitutional reform. It is a sophisticated,
detailed plan, which meets the political aspirations of a
quarter of the nation's people, including all four of the main
ethnic groups.

The area served by this popular, yet revolutionary structure, happens to coincide with one of the development planning regions, the one which contains the homeland of the
Zulu tribes and the rest of the province of Natal. Hence the
KwaZulu Natal Indaba in the title; *Indaba* is a Zulu word for
conference. The plan dates back to the Buthelezi Report, a
document which was prepared some years ago, by Mangosuthu G. Butlelezi, Chief Minister of KwaZulu and President of
Inkatha, before the South African government launched its
most recent constitutional reforms.

It is at once evident from a map that KwaZulu is so intertwined with the rest of Natal, that trying to administer it
adequately, in the style of the government's traditional
homeland policy, has never been possible. The Buthelezi
Commission therefore had to find some governmental structure that could serve the entire region. Investigations began

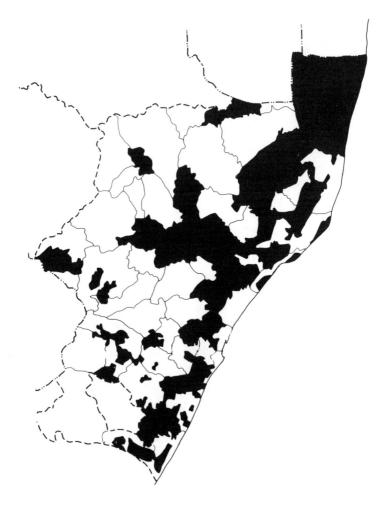

KwaZulu territories within the province of Natal

in 1980, with a large commission of 43 members, representing most community viewpoints.

The final report, in 1981, was ignored for a time; in some quarters it received outright rejection. Then, when the National Government began its major overhaul of the constitution, beginning with the Tricameral Parliament of 1985, there was renewed interest in the Commission's work. Early in 1986, invitations were extended to a wide cross-section of organizations in Natal, asking them to participate in the design of a new constitutional model. Two hundred delegates, representing 34 organizations, accepted; rejections came from the extremes on both sides of the political spectrum: ANC and UDF on one side, CP and Herstigte Nasionale Party (HNP) on the other. The new group met in Durban's City Hall, 03 April, 1986. Almost eight months later, after an extraordinary and successful marathon series of meetings, the participants submitted their report on 28 November.

A good deal of compromise was needed for broad acceptance. It was not possible, for example, to eliminate the defined ethnic groups, and replace them with voluntary groupings, although most would have wished to do that. This limitation was used by UDF opponents to attribute failure to the entire project. They called it a new, thinly-disguised form of apartheid. On the other hand, Lawrence Schlemmer, Director of the Centre for Policy Studies, University of the Witwatersrand, recognized that compromise was its greatest strength. The fact that the ultimate design did not coincide with any one participant's political ideals meant that it belonged to nobody. Given the present degree of political polarization in the country, this factor was a necessary condition for universal acceptance.

The final KwaZulu Natal Indaba document was one which no individual participant was forced to accept, yet everyone was determined to find acceptable solutions. Hence, more than 80 percent of all those involved endorsed the final constitutional proposals as being the best possible under conditions of a free-enterprise economic system. Racial discrimination had no place in it.

There is clear protection of the rights of individuals and groups, the former via a bill of rights, and the latter by means of a two-chamber structure, which ensures maximum sharing of legislative power. A first chamber of 100 members is elected on a one-person-one-vote basis, so that, in all probability, it would be dominated by a Black political party. The second chamber contains 50 members, elected on a basis of choice among five groups, each of which is allocated 10 seats: African, Afrikaans, Asian, English, South African. Voters choose their representatives from one of these five; thus there are two choices, one for the first chamber, and one for a group in the second chamber. The South African group is included for the benefit of those who do not want to recognize ethnicity in the electoral process.

The ten-member cabinet and prime minister, the latter be-

ing the head of the majority party in the first chamber, constitute the executive. Five cabinet members are selected by
the prime minister, the other five by minority parties in both
chambers, with the overall proviso that each of the five
groups in the second chamber be represented in cabinet. All
legislation has to pass through standing committees before
enactment, and those laws which affect the religion, language, or culture of a particular group must be approved by a
majority within that group. The position of the governor, the
titular head of this new, proposed, provincial government,
and the many other facets of the plan, are illustrated in the
accompanying diagram.

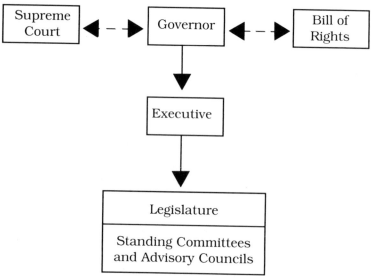

KwaZulu Natal Indaba proposals

Reactions from the National Government have been positive but cautious. First practical recognition came on 07 August, 1987, with the appointment by the State President of
the KwaZulu Natal Joint Executive, the first of its kind in
the history of the nation. This move established a common
secretariat to serve the two authorities. While legislative
powers remained unchanged, there was now a mechanism
for reducing costs, since single instead of double purchasing
and contracting was possible. A second move came later in
the same year, when the Minister of Constitutional Develop-

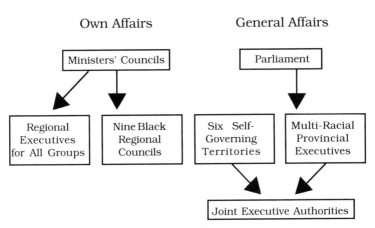

Own Affairs   General Affairs

The New Government (provincial and regional levels)

ment and Planning announced, in Parliament, his support in principle for a single, multi-racial, provincial legislature in Natal.

A survey of 2,000 adults revealed much stronger support for Indaba than was forthcoming from the government. A substantial majority approved. Over 80 percent of the people surveyed had heard about the new constitutional proposal. Predictably, strongest disapproval came from Conservative Party members. The conclusion drawn by the people of Natal is that Whites nationally are more than ready to accept a new brand of negotiation politics.

Against the optimism that pervades the KwaZulu Natal Indaba Joint Executive, there are some major reservations. The minority party has been depicted as the booby prize. There is a possibility of the majority party and the strongest opposition party both being Black. In such a case there could be a majority Black government, with Whites enjoying no more than token representation. Experts agree that this is possible but unlikely; the fact that it is theoretically possible is sufficient to scare off many who would otherwise be supportive. To secure and maintain trust between different ethnic communities is one of the most fundamental challenges facing South Africa.

The Indaba proposal, while designed for one area only, affects much more than Natal. Buthelezi, the architect of the first attempts to structure a new constitution, is also President of Inkatha, a national cultural liberation movement dating back to 1928, but revived and given new status by Buthelezi in 1975. It has a paid membership of well over one million, and 2,500 local branches throughout the country, making it the largest Black political organization in the history of South Africa.

Inkatha's priorities are: Black unity, non-violence, the politics of negotiation, and the promotion of political co-existence across ethnic and racial boundaries. There is a strong and persistent opposition to traditional apartheid, along with a desire to facilitate the development of a democratic and non-racial South Africa. The power base of Inkatha has long been the Zulus because, until recently, there were government regulations which prevented the extension of membership to other Black groups. Now surveys show that almost half of Soweto's Inkatha supporters are non-Zulu.

Perhaps the most important aspect of Inkatha's political outlook is its commitment to a multi-strategy approach. The organization clearly is ready to work with provincial and national White authorities when either presents an opportunity to dismantle apartheid. At the same time, a steady pressure is exercised against all White organizations that seek to maintain discrimination on ethnic or racial lines. Inkatha also works with European and North American agencies, plus organizations across Africa for the same purpose.

Buthelezi's vision is comprehensive and wise. He recognizes the impossibility of confronting the South African government militarily, so he works tirelessly for the unity of the nation's Blacks. He knows that the moral power of a Black majority will be irresistible. Beyond the main goal of equality of opportunity for all, he knows there are other barriers to a better life: poverty, disease, and ignorance. He has not fallen victim to the delusion of revolutionaries, that freedom and wealth will be the lot of everyone, once the government is destroyed and the right people take their place.[56]

It is little wonder that anything in which Buthelezi is involved carries implications for the nation as a whole. Many business and government leaders have already said that the Indaba model, with appropriate modifications, could serve the rest of the country. Buthelezi's influence is further highlighted in his former ties to the African National Congress (ANC). Buthelezi attended Fort Hare University, where

Nelson Mandela also studied, and was part of the ANC, along with Mandela, Oliver Tambo and others before the movement opted for violence.

Over the past 25 years or more, tension has mounted between Inkatha and ANC, partly because of the disagreement over violence, but mainly because the ANC in exile wants to be perceived as the only significant anti-apartheid Black voice. Buthelezi interferes with that ambition. In 1979, a London meeting was arranged between Inkatha and ANC representatives, in an attempt to unite the two organizations. Inkatha was asked to be a surrogate for the ANC within South Africa. Buthelezi refused. Since that time, both Inkatha and the South African government have become targets of ANC terrorism.

ANC agents have tried, again and again, to destabilize Buthelezi and Inkatha in their own backyard, as it were. Strong-arm tactics have been employed to try to prove that the ANC is the sole and authentic voice of Black South Africa, just as had been done in Western countries whenever another South African organization claimed to speak for Blacks. In ANC broadcasts to South Africa from Ethiopia, Buthelezi was described as the snake which is poisoning South Africa, and which needs to be hit on the head.

Hatred of Buthelezi, and everything he stands for, came to a head in 1987, with open warfare in Natal between Inkatha and the ANC surrogate, the UDF. It was a last gasp on the part of the ANC. Its support within South Africa had been steadily diminishing, its visibility only maintained by the name Nelson Mandela, the organization's titular head. Paradoxically, Buthelezi called for Mandela's release from prison as early as the mid-1970s.

The ANC assaults on Inkatha have shown up the inability of this terrorist organization to unite South Africa's Blacks. Inkatha is committed to the same Freedom Charter as the ANC. At an earlier point of time, Buthelezi and Mandela were joint members of the ANC, during the period that it opposed apartheid peacefully. The only policy difference between the two organizations today is whether or not to use violence. These two dominant Black groups thus epitomize the problem facing South African Blacks: how to overcome their ancient habit of inter-tribal conflict and sublimate their bellicose instincts in a common quest for peace.

Parliament Buildings in Umtata, Transkei, the first homeland to gain full independence

16 | Unravelling 1884

*Most of the problems that a President has to face
have their roots in the past.*

Harry S. Truman
Memoirs, 1955

The high point of the European conquest of Africa was
the Berlin Conference of November, 1884. It was a picture of the times. Powerful countries such as Britain,
France, and Germany sat down at a table, thousands of
miles away from the territories under discussion, and carved
out their colonies. Lines were arbitrarily drawn on maps
with no regard to tribal boundaries. The Berlin delegates
were only concerned with their military, economic and political interests. A hundred years later, all over Africa, civil wars
and border conflicts bear eloquent testimony to the permanent damage caused by those colonial decisions.

Present-day outbreaks of violence stem from the retention
of colonial boundaries, in the new African countries, instead
of the historic, tribal demarcation lines. Had the autonomy
of the tribal territories and social structures been asserted in
the newly-independent nations, much of the suffering of the
past quarter century could have been avoided.

Traditional life was hierarchical with the head of the tribe
being the chief. Chiefs were regarded as fathers of their
peoples, custodians of the tribal territories, and upholders of
law and order. They were even expected to get rain in times
of drought, a skill that had special value in the arid regions
of South Africa.

There were other attributes and responsibilities of the
chief that strengthened bonds of obedience and loyalty from
subjects. He regulated the harvest festivals, and served as a
mediator between tribesmen and their ancestral spirits. He

was usually wealthy, because of gifts from other tribes, and fines, confiscations, and gifts from his own people. His wealth became a source of social welfare which, in turn, softened discontent and reduced the risk of revolt.

The position and authority of the chief thus identified the tribe, distinguishing it from all others. All land was communal, held in trust by the chief. There was an annual allotment of arable land and a residential site for each household. The arable land reverted to the chief at the end of harvest, to become part of the common grazing for the winter season.

Within the hierarchical order, after the chief, there were counsellors, each being responsible for several headmen. A headman was the officer in charge of a group of kraals, or dwelling places. Overall, the tribal community formed a single unity with land and social order closely interwoven into a single system. Government and day-to-day decision-making were all part of that system. There was no external authority.

The destruction of that system by colonial authorities, partly by fixing international boundaries that cut into tribal territory, and partly by robbing chiefs of their authority, replacing it with a new form of government, the colonial administrator, effectively destroyed tribal life. Crime, lack of responsibility, and loss of social control ensued. When independence from colonial rule gave way to new African nations, frequently the new governments were no different from those of the colonists. There was no reversion to the kind of consensus local government that had been enjoyed in precolonial times.

The South African government is now making a serious attempt to restore these ancient forms of local government, no longer just for Blacks, but also for the multi-racial societies that, today, occupy so many places. The new form of local government is known as regional services councils. It is the latest stage of the new local governments that were first introduced in 1978, and it provides for both consensus decision-making and redistribution of wealth at the community level, where the effects are felt immediately and directly.

After 1910, the year of formation of the Union of South Africa, the government maintained a British-style colonial administration, similar to those which operated at that time in Australia, Canada, and New Zealand. Over the years there were major changes in the status of these countries, such as the 1931 Statute of Westminster which provided complete autonomy for all four nations. This British tradition of parliamentary rule, with the Queen as Sovereign, was the form of government in South Africa for 50 years following union.

In 1958, Dr. H. F. Verwoerd became Prime Minister of South Africa and new priority was given to the policy of separate development, or apartheid as it was first described by the British in the 1930s. This led to severe tensions within the Commonwealth, to which South Africa still belonged, such that, in 1961, the country withdrew its membership and declared itself to be a republic.

Events followed in swift succession: a new citizenship act removed the term 'British Subject'; the rights of citizens to appeal to the British Privy Council were abolished; the British anthem and flag were downgraded; and the British naval base at Simonstown was taken over by the South African Navy.

The roots of past governments can be seen in the South African flag and in the present locations of the main government and judicial institutions. The flag is a four-fold reminder of the major influences which shaped the country: Dutch, British, Orange Free State and Transvaal. Parliament's location in Cape Town, the Judiciary in Bloemfontein, and the administrative capital in Pretoria all reflect the desire to restore unity following the conflicts between British and Afrikaners.

As long as South Africa was a member of the Commonwealth, the understanding with Britain was that the protectorates of Bechuanaland, Basutoland, and Swaziland, now known as Botswana, Lesotho and Swaziland respectively, would form part of South Africa. Had this plan materialized, complaints over the distribution of land as between Whites and Blacks would never have arisen. More than half of South Africa would have been allocated to the Black states. Britain, however, changed her mind soon after 1961, and arranged independence for these three homelands without South Africa's consent.

Looking back now on the fateful decisions of the 1960s, when the concept of completely separate Black states crystallized, it must have been impossible for the leaders of that time to anticipate the changed thinking of later years. There was every reason to assume that local and world communities would accept the pattern of nation-states which had already emerged from homelands in Botswana, Lesotho, and Swaziland.

South Africa retained the British parliamentary form of government, essentially unchanged, from 1961 to 1985. Then, on 25 January 1985, under a new constitution, came South Africa's first Tricameral, or three-part, Parliament, which included Whites, Coloreds, and Indians. The new structure is a unique combination of a strong presidential system, like that of France, and a three-way British-style parliament. Each of the three houses has full responsibility for matters affecting its own affairs and a shared responsibility for general, or national affairs. In practice, the approach to legislation emphasizes consensus via joint committees.

The exclusion of Blacks from the new Parliament created a fresh wave of opposition to the policy of national states. The world community refused to recognize the new states, while more and more Blacks chose to stay out of their homelands, preferring to live in the segregated townships on the outskirts of the big cities. An entirely new approach was needed to a governmental role for Blacks in national affairs.

Early in the 1980s, as a result of these developments, the South African government scrapped the entire concept of totally separate development and introduced sweeping changes to the existing laws: common citizenship for all South Africans including, if they so wished, the four states that had already chosen independence; freedom to marry across racial lines; common access for all groups to the various institutions of society, and freehold land rights for Blacks in so-called White areas; abolition of pass books; a new policy of urbanization in place of the traditional influx controls; introduction of a political structure for the involvement of Blacks at the national level; replacement of provincial White legislatures by multi-racial executives; and, at local levels, the regional services councils (RSCs).

RSCs are miniature tricameral parliaments, except that they do not represent a new level of government. They coordinate the work of local authorities and so reduce costs via economies of scale. Like Parliament, they sometimes have to look after general affairs that affect Asians, Blacks, Coloreds, and Whites, through activities that impinge on local governments in all four ethnic areas; at other times, they may be involved in one local government, dealing with that government's own affairs. Typically, RSCs will coordinate work in

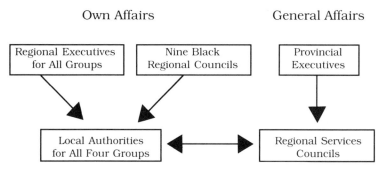

The New Government (local level)

such things as water, sewage, electricity, roads, health, markets, safety, and leisure facilities. These new councils are presently operating in the Johannesburg area, Pretoria, Port Elizabeth, Cape Town, Bloemfontein, and Walvis Bay. Their territorial limits are set by provincial authorities.

As coordinating agencies only, RSCs would not represent anything new in restoring responsibility and self respect to Blacks. Fortunately there is more to their function than economic efficiency. They can levy taxes through pay roll deductions, the amounts based on a percentage of wages. They can also tax business enterprises and this kind of revenue has become their main source of income. With these moneys, and under the laws enacted for RSCs, the former modes of consensus decision-making could be restored.

The new moneys must be allocated, consistently, to the areas of greatest need. This means the Black areas in most cases, yet most of the money will come from White sources. Wealth must be taken from the richer areas to raise standards in the poorer urban sections. To ensure that this policy is not circumvented by the richer local authorities ganging-up on the poorer ones, there is a stipulation that no ethnic group can have more than 50 percent voting power in an RSC, and a two-thirds majority vote is required for all decisions. In one RSC, that of Central Witwatersrand, more than US$30 million was spent in one recent year, all but $500,000 of which was given to Black areas.

The value to Blacks of an agency of this kind is incalculable. They are involved for the first time in identifying, along with other ethnic representatives, the greatest needs in the total community, and they have to learn to arrive at a single decision, not a majority vote. The process is very similar to ancient tribal bargaining, where no one has absolute power, but where give-and-take leads to a decision acceptable to all. Human relationships are improved in so doing, and the sense of community is heightened.

There have been the usual criticisms of RSCs from those quasi-leadership cliques that see everything in terms of political ideology. They refuse to support any arrangement that is not based on voluntary groups. Other opposition organizations accept these ethnic categories as necessary, interim arrangements. In either case, it is increasingly clear that pragmatism, rather than ideology, will dominate the thinking of South Africans for many years to come.

Many Black leaders have said they need help from Whites in order to develop the skills necessary for self-government, especially in large urban areas. Local government, and especially RSCs, provide the kind of experience they need. One Black leader has called RSCs nurseries of democracy. His statement is true for almost all Blacks; unfortunately, only the poor, uneducated, large majority know that this is so.

While RSCs are harbingers of multi-racial communities, similar things are happening at the scale of the individual. In Krugersdorp, a major industrial, farming, and communication centre, twenty miles north-west of Johannesburg, a White family adopted Emelia, a homeless Black child, and gave her the full freedom that any White child would normally enjoy.

The event might not have been noticed in most parts of South Africa. The legal structures that are supposed to separate Blacks from Whites have been eroding in recent years and shared patterns of living are becoming commonplace. The significance of Emelia is the location of her story. Krugersdorp is heartland South Africa, a place steeped in history. Close by, over one hundred years ago, the South African Republic, now the Transvaal, was proclaimed. Here are found both the conservative and liberal extremes of Afrikaner ideology. If there is going to be national acceptance of a multi-racial society, Krugersdorp might well be the touchstone of the national will.

The farming couple that adopted Emelia was not prepared for the storm that ensued. When Emelia went to church, some members of the local Dutch Reformed Church were outraged, and threatened to resign. Others welcomed the child. Telephone callers from the community were also divided in their opinions. Many were supportive, some indicating that they, too, had adopted homeless Black children without telling others. The emotional intensity resulting from this incident was a reflection of the country's polarization. By highlighting the historical differences between South Africa's two main races, Emelia became the national debate in miniature.

South Africa's State President P. W. Botha

17 | Beyond Apartheid: One United Nation

Heaven is not reached at a single bound.

Josiah G. Holland
Gradatim, 1872

The year 1983 was a turning point in South Africa's political life. The White electorate gave a resounding "Yes" to the question: should Coloreds and Indians be included in the parliamentary system? It was probably the first time in history that a minority in power decided, freely, to share power, and also the first time since 1956 that national-level political power was extended to non-Whites. To State President P. W. Botha it represented a major step toward national unity.

In the years that followed, the pace of change accelerated. At the same time, widespread unrest broke out in a number of areas, partly a result of the omission of Blacks from the new constitution, partly because of an economic recession, leading to a rise in unemployment. The recession was, to some extent, a result of internationally-imposed economic sanctions. Excessive optimism, and the resultant frustration when hopes were not met, was yet another factor. This was how the State President described the new dispensation at the opening of Parliament in 1985:

> I confirm that my Party and I are committed to the principle of a united South Africa, one citizenship and a universal franchise within structures chosen by South Africans. . . . It is evident that units will have to be recognized on a geographical and group basis. This includes the Black urban communities who, for constitutional purposes, are recognized as political entities. Each unit should have autonomy on matters that affect that unit only, while all units jointly manage common

concerns at the central level. . . . We are involved in the pursuance of both equal rights for individuals and security for each group. The ways in which fundamental individual and group rights are protected are therefore essential elements of constitutional reform. . . . We must accept dual citizenship for those Black governments that have chosen independence, should they so wish.

Three brand-new tiers of government emerged, each multi-racial in constitution. The third level was the regional services councils, the second, provincial, but not in the traditional sense of the word. The Whites-only governments that had controlled Cape Province, Natal, Orange Free State, and the Transvaal were abolished. In their places the State President appointed multi-racial executives who are directly responsible to Parliament, which now exercises legislative control on behalf of the four provinces. The first tier was the Tricameral Parliament, with its new form of government executive.

A reform movement of the kind initiated in 1983, in the context of South Africa's divided society, is fraught with enormous difficulties. To begin with, it is not the ideal arrangement, since the initiative has to be entirely on the side of the government. A negotiated constitution, in which all South Africans participated, would be much better and is, in fact, the long-term government policy.

Negotiation has to wait for the time when all parties are persuaded that it is the best way. Under widespread international support for revolution, it is hard to convince young terrorists that they can't gain their ends by force. They have been told by so many, and supported by such large amounts of money from Soviet and other sources, that they understandably feel confident, assured of final victory. Professor Albert P. Blaustein, international authority on constitutional design, pointed out the folly of this kind of thinking:

> The South African constitution cannot be imposed from outside, neither by well-meaning foreign liberals in America and Europe, properly opposed to apartheid, nor by the Marxist ideologues of refugee liberation groups. . . . A constitution must be home-grown; it must spring from the soil. It must be bespoke, custom-made to meet the needs, wants, and aspirations of the peoples for whom it is written.[57]

A second difficulty facing reform stems from the currency being given to one-man-one-vote in a unitary state, often

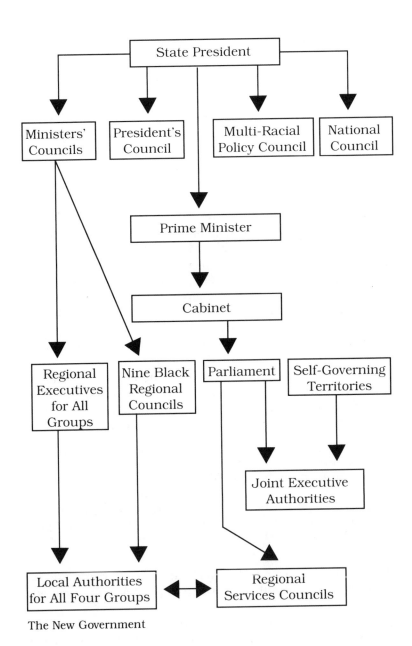

The New Government

called the Westminster, winner-take-all model. This style of administration is a recent arrival in the long history of government, yet it has been universally promoted as the epitome of democracy to new, post-colonial nations. South Africa is thereby identified as a nation opposed to democracy. Yet consensus politics has been the most enduring style of government in the long history of human society. More recently, in the face of disastrous experiences with the Westminster model in Africa and elsewhere, a new emphasis is being given to consensus politics. Even in Europe, the horror of majority tyranny is seen in divided societies such as Northern Ireland and Cyprus.

In fragmented, grouped societies, such as those found all over Africa, Latin America, and Asia, the Westminster model destroys democracy. In a group that is sharply separated from others by language, religion, standard of living, and authority structure, people tend to espouse the same political point of view. In Africa, this means block voting along tribal lines. The biggest tribe becomes the permanent government, and all smaller tribes are permanently excluded.

In 1980, the choice of new leaders in Rhodesia, leading to the nation of Zimbabwe, was one of the most carefully supervised elections in the history of Africa. An analysis of votes shows that 90 percent of the Shonas, the largest tribal group, voted for Robert Mugabe, the Shona leader, while the same proportion of the minority Ndebele voted for their leader. About 20 years earlier, in 1965, A. J. A. Peck, from Salisbury, Rhodesia, wrote as follows to the London *Times*:

> Mr. [Harold] Wilson's grandiloquent phrase "majority rule" is a terminological inexactitude masquerading in the purple robes of a Pontius Pilate. Mr. Wilson well knows that in Ghana there is no "majority rule": one man rules—Dr. Nkrumah; he well knows the position to be the same in numerous other African states; and he well knows that "majority rule" in Rhodesia would today, inevitably, bring dictatorship by one particular man.[58]

Mugabe became Prime Minister. Within a few years, and after brutal persecution of the minority Ndebele tribe, he made himself dictator.

Reform is a slow painstaking process. There is none of the glamor of revolution. Those in the existing order experience frustration because their positions are undermined. To the idealist, reform is meaningless; the dream encompasses only a glorious new world where all wrongs are put right. Reforming a complex system by stages, ignoring many inequities simply because only a few things can be done at one time, leaves the reformer open to criticism from people who hold other priorities. The parallel at the human scale is a person trying to make improvements on an old house when it would be so much easier to build a new, albeit much more costly home.

Often, only one item of reform can be tackled at a given time. The power-base of the initiator may have to be convinced of the value of what is planned, then people have to be persuaded of the benefits, before research, parliamentary discussion and legislation complete the process. All this takes time, with the result that subsequent reforms are announced at widely-spaced intervals. People, unless they are following developments with great care, forget the earlier changes. Outside the country, observers who do not understand the difficulties accuse the government of stalling, or else they describe each move as cosmetic; nevertheless, despite the cynicism from North Americans and other Westerners, there is recognition within South Africa, from Blacks and Whites alike, that worthwhile changes are taking place.

There is strong opposition to reform within South Africa from those who are determined to maintain the privileged position of Whites. Experience in the United States, after the Civil War of 1861 to 1865, illustrates a comparable situation. The victorious North had occupied the conquered territory of the South after the War. The total U.S. population at that time was approximately the same as that of South Africa today.

American Blacks were being given the right to vote for the first time. Many Whites objected. The more extreme formed secret societies, such as the Ku Klux Klan, to resist change and to maintain White supremacy. At the same time, political stresses appeared in the central government, between the President and the different parties in Congress, as to whether or not reparations were to be demanded of the defeated states. These stresses, coupled with the difficulties of gaining adequate support in the South, often delayed the transfer of power back to the state legislatures for as much as seven years. Even then, it was only a beginning. The mature expression of the Black franchise had to wait for another one hundred years.

The parallels in South Africa are easy to see. There is a strong minority among Whites that is resisting all attempts to bring Blacks into national politics. They have already secured membership in the central government, and there are continuing stresses at that level whenever there is legislation that moves the nation toward a multi-racial society. The need for time is apparent. Hopefully it will not take seven years to put the basic structures in place, nor a further hundred before the country sees the full expression of political rights and responsibilities.

There is a continuing quest for a new constitution, parallelling the reform process. Whatever the shape of the final design, all the changes that are now taking place will help in the transition period, since they include joint decision-making across ethnic lines. One proposal copies the Swiss Canton system. It is an extreme form of decentralization, advocated by leaders in the business community, because of its inherent suitability for free-enterprise economics.

The Swiss Constitution developed over a long period of time. As each community joined with others to form a national unit, the individual cantons retained most of the powers generally accorded a central government. As a result, the national authority had little more to do that deal with foreign and other external-related affairs. In the transfer of this model to South Africa, some three hundred communes are proposed, each of which would be free to choose its own political and economic system. There would even be a right of secession from South Africa.

There are many objections to the plan. Like Blaustein, a majority feels that the kind of constitution needed for South Africa will be unique. It cannot be imported; it must be home-grown. Many argue that the sudden abolition of tribal, and other forms of group identity, would create unacceptable stresses in a small community, leading to the smothering of minority rights. The biggest problem relates to the process of implementation. If the different ethnic groups cannot get together around a negotiating table to hammer out a new constitution, how could such a detailed, interdependent form of government be introduced?

The Tricameral Parliament, provincial multi-racial executives, regional services councils, plus reforms, significant and far-reaching as they are, still leave unanswered the problem of bringing Blacks into the central government. Early in 1986, State President P. W. Botha introduced the National Statutory Council, an agency to serve as a first step to power sharing at the national level. Terms of reference for the Council were deliberately vague, so that delegates from the homelands and urban townships could meet with government representatives and jointly decide on an agenda.

There were threats of violence in a few places against any Black leader who decided to participate in the new council. One homeland leader refused to get involved until Nelson Mandela was released from prison. Still others were opposed to any arrangement that did not allow for voluntary, rather than racially-defined groups. These difficulties compelled the government to provide some structure for the Council. In 1988, a new, more prescriptive, National Council Bill was presented to Parliament by the State President.

Its membership consists of approximately equal numbers of Blacks and Whites: cabinet ministers and others nominated by the State President, representatives of the six self-governing national states or homelands, together with representatives of the Black communities outside the national states. The four independent national states (Bophuthatswana, Ciskei, Transkei, and Venda) are excluded, but they are involved at national level through regular conferences with the government. In order to represent the non-homeland, mainly urban Blacks, the nine economic development regions have been taken as geographical units, and Black local councillors, within each of these regions, elect delegates to the Council. Each representative group, in turn, nominates the chairman.

Two major governmental changes have been made since the Council was first launched, both of them designed to provide greater participation for Blacks at the highest levels of national life. Elected Black authorities, with provincial powers, have been instituted in each of the nine economic development regions. A new, multi-racial, policy-making body, headed by the State President, has been established to deal with critical issues of national policy, such as economics, social concerns, finance, security, and foreign affairs.

One implication of the new government changes is the possibility of a fourth chamber, for Blacks, to parallel the three existing ones for Asians, Coloreds and Whites. The absence of a fourth chamber in the 1984 Constitution led to

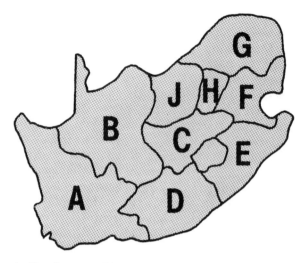

Economic Development Planning Regions

widespread suspicion among Blacks that they would never be given a role in the national parliament. Clearly, whether or not that is the case, Blacks have already been given a role at the national level alongside other ethnic groups. Under the 1988 changes, Blacks can be nominated to the President's Council or to the Cabinet, and can participate directly in the election of the head of state. It is inevitable that a Black will ultimately become State President under this system.

Crossing all lines of political structures are the classifications of own affairs and general affairs. The former refers to the interests and responsibilities of specific ethnic groups such as Colored or Black. Throughout the nation's long history, each one of the four ethnic groups has created or was given its own institutions for such services as education, local government, and public health, and these services have been developed in the locations where the members of the group live. Conversely, the general affairs classification concerns the institutions that serve the total community, such as civil law, national defence, and foreign relations. At the local level of government, own affairs and general affairs have been brought together into a working partnership through the regional services councils. The unfinished task is the creation of a similar partnership at the national level.

Cost remains an unyielding problem in all these plans. At the very moment in history when governments everywhere are calling for reductions in their structures and responsibilities, it seems that South Africa is calling for more government. However, such a perception may not be accurate. Many suggest that the real purpose of the recent additions to government relates to flexibility. In order to achieve a constitution acceptable to all, it is essential to test alternative designs thoroughly. In so doing, Blacks and other ethnic groups will feel free to propose their own agendas in the quest for an agreed formula.

The desired outcome from these changes, however long it may take to achieve it, is the same as the one envisaged at the beginning of 1986: the drafting of a brand-new constitution which brings people from all ethnic communities into the national government, a constitution that is acceptable to the vast majority of South Africans. Earlier, State President Botha stressed that he was not interested in perpetuating the structures of apartheid which he inherited in 1978. The system of racial and tribal compartmentalization by which South Africa is administered, he said, "is not a policy—it is a social reality; reform is our policy."[59] By the year 2000, if changes continue at their present rate, the reform program and the National Council's work will have been completed, presenting a challenge to the critics and a new harmony among South Africans.

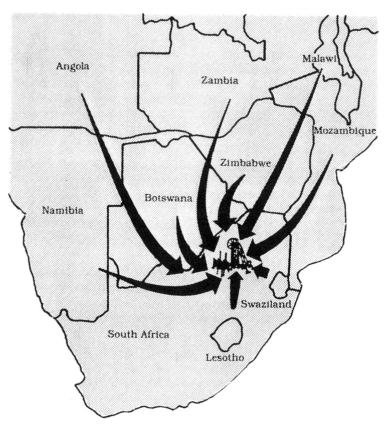

Workers from neighboring countries employed in South Africa

18 | African Neighbors

Better is a neighbor that is near than a brother far off.

Proverbs 27:10

The African countries that lie below latitude 10 degrees South form a well-defined region, that of Southern Africa. It is the second smallest of the continent's five geo-economic regions, with regard to both population and surface area, and it is home to ten nations: Angola, Botswana, Lesotho, Malawi, Mozambique, Namibia, South Africa, Swaziland, Zambia, and Zimbabwe. Ninety million people live here, representing 15 percent of Africa's 1988 total.

The ties that link these nations together date back to colonial times. In the heyday of the British Empire, Botswana, Lesotho, Malawi, South Africa, Swaziland, Zambia, and Zimbabwe all formed a single political unit. Railways and roads were built, and patterns of trade evolved, to serve the seven colonies as if they were a single country. South Africa, by far the wealthiest of these colonies, was the communications hub, a function it has retained throughout the twentieth century. Until tensions developed over its policies of separate development, South Africa supported a high degree of regional cooperation which strengthened and expanded these traditional ties.

There is little formal cooperation at the present time. Malawi is the only one of nine neighbors that has normal diplomatic relations with South Africa. However, while the formal ties are few, the reality of mutual cooperation is quite a different story. Most of the imports and exports of Malawi, Zambia and Zimbabwe are carried to and from South Afri-

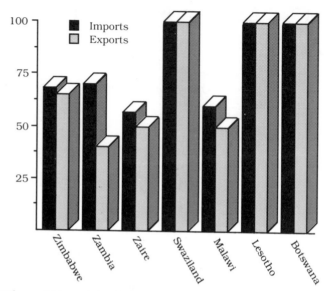

Southern African interdependence

Percentage of each nation's total
exports and imports carried by
SATS (South African Transport Services)

can ports on South African railways. Daily communication
and various institutional relationships are essential if one's
level of dependence is of this order.

Responsibility for repairs, provision of spare parts, and
technical assistance, in almost all aspects of the region's
transportation system, falls on South Africa. There are trade
offices in more than a dozen countries, secretly arranging
business transactions for virtually all of the continent. Already South Africa's trade surplus with Africa is running at
more than US$1.5 billion annually. The economic ties were
once typified in the phrase: if South Africa sneezes, the rest
of Sub-Sahara Africa gets a cold, if not influenza. Some
80,000 businessmen, from 45 African nations, visited South
Africa in 1987 to firm up business deals. Johannesburg has
become the continent's New York.

It is easy to see why there are close economic ties. South
Africa produces 80% of Southern Africa's total GNP, 77% of
its electricity, 87% of the wheat, 97% of coal, 98% of iron ore,

and 67% of the sugar cane crop. Additionally, South Africa undertakes massive construction projects in neighboring countries, like the Lesotho Highlands Water Project, and the modernization of Maputo harbor.

In one assistance project, South Africa agreed to subsidize Botswana through buying bulk quantities of its soda ash, although this action would mean loss of business for a U.S. company which exported soda ash to South Africa. The U.S. company, backed by its government, threatened to go to court on the grounds of a breach of international trading agreements. The U.S. was willing to hurt Botswana in order to maintain its own sales to South Africa while, simultaneously, persisting with its anti-apartheid sanctions in flagrant violation of international trading agreements.[60]

Durban harbor is the centre of activity for the export and import trade of many Southern African countries. The tonnage of cargo passing through this port increases year by year. In addition, there is a constant flow of oil coming into the country via Durban, building up the country's reserves. These tankers arrive at night and leave in the morning before daylight.

Agriculture is by far the most critical aspect of South Africa's relations with the rest of the continent. There has been a serious decline in Africa's agricultural production. The World Bank identifies the continent as the only major region of the world where food production is losing the race with population growth. This neglect of farming is due to several factors: low social prestige accorded agricultural pursuits, with the result that subsistence farming is being widely neglected; low priority by governments; a history of dependence on grain that is donated by Western countries. South Africa regularly exports corn, the staple diet of so many people, to more than a dozen nations.

In addition to the trade and communications ties, there are also the many human interactions. Half a million workers from Southern African countries regularly earn a living in the South African mines. There are also hundreds of thousands of illegal immigrants. Recently, under the pressure of Western sanctions, some of these miners have been repatriated to Mozambique. The East German government has taken 8,000 of these unemployed people to Leipzig to work in the brown coal mines. Results have been far from satisfactory. The Mozambiquans hate the climate, resent the racism from locals, and complain bitterly that they are being paid less than they received from South Africa.[61]

Violence has erupted between the Mozambiquans and mining communities with casualties on both sides. One reason for local hostility is fear of contracting the AIDS virus. The end result is a petition from the Mozambiquans to be allowed to return, not only to their homeland, but also to their former jobs in South Africa.

In an attempt to escape from their dependence on South Africa, several neighboring countries have tried to find alternative railway routes. The results have been disastrous. The Tazara line to Dar-es-Salaam, Tanzania, has been plagued with administrative inefficiency. Less than a third of the locomotives are in working order; goods pile up at the dockside. In Mozambique the situation is equally disappointing. Revolutionaries seeking to overthrow their government regularly knock the line to Beira out of commission. At present, 12,000 soldiers from Zimbabwe, who guard this line, usually prevent sabotage; however, the general inefficiency and frequent breakdowns persist, with the result that everything is behind schedule. The Benguela line in Angola is effectively immobilised by the National Union for the Total Independence of Angola (UNITA), a group fighting the government of that country.

The shrill anti-apartheid rhetoric of South Africa's neighbors makes little sense. Their statements of willingness to accept the hardships implicit in full-scale sanctions make even less sense. In 1987 a Commonwealth Report recognized the failure of frontline states to impose sanctions. It should be noted, however, that political expediency demands that these declarations be made. The Lusaka Manifesto of 1969, which recommended the violent overthrow of the present government, led to huge gifts of money for impoverished Zambia from misguided Western governments. It is just as necessary to distinguish public posturing from reality in the Black countries surrounding South Africa as it is in those Black communities within the country.

Zambia happens to be a good example of the tightly knit, indissoluble relationships that characterize so many of the countries of Southern Africa. Here are some examples of its dependency on South Africa: borrowed money; transportation of its exports and imports; supplies of various manufactured goods, telecommunications equipment, rolling stock, and mining equipment; various forms of technical assistance; food; scientific assistance in the fields of meteorology, veterinary surgery, and research; tourism; air links.

Saddest of all elements affecting the region is war. Over the past twenty-five years, Southern Africa has experienced an enormous amount of tension and conflict. All through the 1960s and 1970s more than half of the nations have been embroiled in armed struggle of one kind or another. A worldwide focus of interest has accompanied these events, with a special concentration on Angola, where the presence of Cuban troops involved the superpowers.

Beginning in the early 1960s Angola was launched into a civil war that still continues, in spite of the independence that was secured in 1974. Portugal transferred power to a coalition of former revolutionary parties. Almost immediately afterward there was dissension among the parties and civil war resumed. The Popular Movement for the Liberation of Angola (MPLA), aided by the Cubans, won out, and has held on to power ever since.

The story in Mozambique was similar. A coalition was formed to ensure the transfer of power from the Government of Portugal. In the ensuing struggle, the Front for the Liberation of Mozambique (FRELIMO) emerged the victor. Again, as in Angola, civil war resumed.

In Zimbabwe the situation was different from other colonial territories. The ruling party that had been part of the colonial administration declared independence from Britain in 1965. Guerrilla warfare broke out soon afterward and continued right up to the time of independence in 1976. The Zimbabwe African National Union (ZANU), was the group that finally secured power. Just prior to independence, ZANU had the additional support of newly independent Mozambique. As in other countries of the region, independence did not ensure peace. There was trouble with a rival tribe, leading to bloodshed and a shift to one-party rule.

In other nations the transition to independence was marked by similar fratricidal strife. Lesotho's independence from Britain in 1966 was followed four years later by a bloody civil war which was won by the Basutoland National Party (BNP). Southwest Africa, or Namibia, a former German colony and a South African mandate since World War I, has been the scene of trans-border conflicts between the South-west African Peoples Organization (SWAPO), based in Angola, and the South African Defence Forces.

Present conditions in the ten nations of Southern Africa are summarized below:[62]

Angola

Area in million km^2	1.2
Percentage of land arable	3
Population in millions	9.2
Annual population growth rate (%)	2.8
Urban population in millions	25
Annual urban growth rate (%)	5.7
Capital	Luanda
Currency	Kwanza
Language	Portuguese
Main export	Oil
Passenger cars per 1,000 people	20
Telephones per 1,000 people	6
Radios per 1,000 people	20
Percentage of population literate	25
Average annual income per person (US$)	470

Botswana

Area in million km^2	0.6
Percentage of land arable	2
Population in millions	1.2
Annual population growth rate (%)	3.5
Urban population in millions	16
Annual urban growth rate (%)	7.9
Capital	Gaborone
Currency	Pula
Languages	Setswana, English
Main export	Diamonds
Passenger cars per 1,000 people	10
Telephones per 1,000 people	15
Radios per 1,000 people	116
Percentage of population literate	63
Average annual income per person (US$)	840

Lesotho

Area in million km²	0.03
Percentage of land arable	10
Population in millions	1.7
Annual population growth rate (%)	2.5
Urban population in millions	6
Annual urban growth rate (%)	7.1
Capital	Maseru
Currency	Loti
Languages	Sesotho, English
Main exports	Diamonds, Wool
Passenger cars per 1,000 people	3
Telephones per 1,000 people	4
Radios per 1,000 people	28
Percentage of population literate	64
Average annual income per person (US$)	480

Malawi

Area in million km²	0.1
Percentage of land arable	25
Population in millions	7.7
Annual population growth rate (%)	3.4
Urban population in millions	11
Annual urban growth rate (%)	7.7
Capital	Lilongwe
Currency	Kwacha
Languages	Chichewa, English
Main exports	Tobacco, Tea
Passenger cars per 1,000 people	3
Telephones per 1,000 people	5
Radios per 1,000 people	46
Percentage of population literate	30
Average annual income per person (US$)	170

Mozambique

Area in million km²	0.8
Percentage of land arable	4
Population in millions	15
Annual population growth rate (%)	3.6
Urban population in millions	11
Annual urban growth rate (%)	6.7
Capital	Maputo
Currency	Metical
Language	Portuguese
Main exports	Prawns, nuts
Passenger cars per 1,000 people	8
Telephones per 1,000 people	4
Radios per 1,000 people	25
Percentage of population literate	35
Average annual income per person (US$)	270

Namibia

Area in million km²	0.8
Percentage of land arable	1
Population in millions	1.3
Annual population growth rate (%)	3
Urban population in millions	26
Annual urban growth rate (%)	5.7
Capital	Windhoek
Currency	Rand
Languages	Afrikaans, English
Main exports	Uranium, diamonds
Passenger cars per 1,000 people	50
Telephones per 1,000 people	56
Radios per 1,000 people	46
Percentage of population literate	68
Average annual income per person (US$)	1520

South Africa

Area in million km²	1.2
Percentage of land arable	11
Population in millions	37
Annual population growth rate (%)	2.6
Urban population in millions	52
Annual urban growth rate (%)	3.8
Capital	Pretoria/ Cape Town
Currency	Rand
Languages	Afrikaans, English
Main exports	Gold, minerals
Passenger cars per 1,000 people	86
Telephones per 1,000 people	118
Radios per 1,000 people	274
Percentage of population literate	76
Average annual income per person (US$)	2010

Swaziland

Area in million km²	0.02
Percentage of land arable	8
Population in millions	0.9
Annual population growth rate (%)	3.5
Urban population in millions	10
Annual urban growth rate (%)	5.8
Capital	Mbabane
Currency	Lilangeni
Languages	Siswati, English
Main exports	Sugar, wood
Passenger cars per 1,000 people	25
Telephones per 1,000 people	22
Radios per 1,000 people	152
Percentage of population literate	55
Average annual income per person (US$)	650

Zambia

Area in million km^2	0.8
Percentage of land arable	7
Population in millions	7.4
Annual population growth rate (%)	3.2
Urban population in millions	42
Annual urban growth rate (%)	5.3
Capital	Lusaka
Currency	Kwacha
Language	English
Main export	Copper
Passenger cars per 1,000 people	17
Telephones per 1,000 people	10
Radios per 1,000 people	26
Percentage of population literate	60
Average annual income per person (US$)	400

Zimbabwe

Area in million km^2	0.4
Percentage of land arable	7
Population in millions	9.3
Annual population growth rate (%)	3.5
Urban population in millions	27
Annual urban growth rate (%)	6.2
Capital	Harare
Currency	Dollar
Language	English
Main exports	Tobacco, gold
Passenger cars per 1,000 people	30
Telephones per 1,000 people	30
Radios per 1,000 people	40
Percentage of population literate	70
Average annual income per person (US$)	650

In 1984 there was a dramatic shift from the litany of tension and strife throughout the southern part of Africa. Mozambique and South Africa, under the twin pressures of a severe drought and an accompanying economic recession, laid aside the luxury of ideological differences and signed a peace and security pact. The incursions of members of the African National Congress (ANC) into South Africa from bases in Mozambique, were to be stopped. Similarly, South African support for anti-government forces within Mozambique was to end. Some members of the Organization of African Unity (OAU) saw the agreement as a betrayal of the struggle against the South African government. Others perceived South Africa as the new peacemaker. Whatever the long term outcome of this development, it proved that there are alternatives to violence.

Events

A page of history is worth a volume of logic.

Oliver Wendell Holmes Jr.

1488	Bartolomeu Dias lands at Mossel Bay
1652	First settlement at Cape Town under van Riebeeck
1688	French Huguenot settlers arrive
1713	Smallpox epidemic among Khoikhoi
1795	First British occupation
1806	Second British occupation
1812	Colonial troops force Blacks east of Fish River
1820	Five thousand British settlers arrive at Eastern Cape
1836	Great Boer Trek from the Cape
1838	Battle of Blood River
	Republic of Natal founded by trekkers
1843	Natal annexed by British authorities
1852	Independence of the Afrikaner South African Republic
1854	Independence of the Afrikaner Orange Free State
1860	Indian laborers introduced into Natal
1867	Discovery of diamonds on the Orange Free State border
1868	British annex Basutoland
1871	British annex diamond fields
1872	Cape Colony granted responsible government
1877	British annex the Transvaal
1880	First Anglo-Boer War
1881	The Transvaal declared independent
1884	Gold discovered at Barberton
1885	Railway from Cape Town to Kimberley completed
1886	Rand gold wealth discovered
1892	Johannesburg connected to Cape railway system

1893	Natal granted responsible government
1894	Johannesburg connected by rail to Delagoa Bay
1895	Failure of the Jameson Raid
1898	Paul Kruger elected Transvaal President for fourth time
1899	Outbreak of second Anglo-Boer War
1904	Chinese labor introduced into the gold mines
1910	Union of South Africa formed
1913	Natives Land Act passed
1915	Capture of German Southwest Africa
1919	South African mandate over Southwest Africa
1922	Strikes and revolutionary activities on the Rand
1925	Afrikaans declared one of the two official languages
1930	Franchise given to white women
1948	Nationalist government comes to power
1961	South Africa leaves the Commonwealth
1962	ANC begins revolutionary violence against government
1966	Dr. H. F. Verwoerd assassinated
1968	Malawi/South Africa establish diplomatic relations
1976	Transkei independence
1977	Bophuthatswana independence
1978	P. W. Botha becomes Prime Minister
1979	Venda independence
1981	Ciskei independence
1984	Peace accord with Mozambique at Nkomati
1986	Government repeals 'apartheid-type' laws
1987	Common citizenship for South Africans of all races
1988	Creation of multi-racial policy-making body for national affairs

Glossary

African National Congress (ANC) Originally a peaceful protest movement; since 1960 a banned organization operating outside the country, committed to the violent overthrow of the present South African government.

Afrikaans One of South Africa's two official languages.

Afrikaners The descendants of the first Europeans to settle in South Africa.

Afrikaner Broederbond Afrikaans for Band of Brothers. A society formed after World War I to promote the economic advancement of Afrikaners.

Afrikaner, Jonker Hottentot leader who controlled most of Angola, Namibia, and Botswana for the first half of the nineteenth century.

Afrikaner Reformed Church A breakaway minority within the Dutch Reformed Church which maintains a Whites-only community.

Afrikaner Volkswag Afrikaans for People's Guard. An organization set up in 1983 to uphold as non-negotiable the principle of a White state. Strongly supported by the Conservative Party.

Alexandra A Black township in the suburbs of Johannesburg.

Amandla Zulu for Power is Ours.

Anglo-American Corporation One of South Africa's biggest manufacturing companies. Founded in 1917 by Ernest Oppenheimer.

Anglo-Boer War I *See* Boer War I.

Anglo-Boer War II *See* Boer War II.

Angola A country lying north of Namibia. Formerly a Portuguese Colony. Since independence in 1974 it has experienced continuous civil war. It serves as a base for terrorist incursions into Namibia.

Angora goat   An animal reared in the Eastern Cape, mainly for its valuable mohair.

Apartheid   Afrikaans word meaning separate development. Over time it has come to mean the policies of the present South African government.

Asians   Within South Africa, the term refers almost exclusively to the East Indian population of Natal.

Assegai   A short, stabbing spear developed by the Zulu King Shaka.

Athlone   A Colored township near Cape Town.

Attridgeville   A Black township near Pretoria.

Azania   Used by the Greeks to describe all land south of Egypt. Adopted by the Pan-Africanist Congress, a banned, revolutionary organization like the ANC, as its name for South Africa.

Azanian People's Organization (AZAPO)   The Black Consciousness Movement founded in 1978.

BAAS   Afrikaans word for master. Frequently used by Blacks with reference to a White supervisor.

Baasskap   Afrikaans for boss-ship. Used as a symbol of authority.

Banning   Government order limiting the political and social activities of individuals and organizations that are considered a danger to public order.

Bantu   General descriptive term for the Black tribes that migrated southward to South Africa. Latterly, because of a perception that it was derogatory, the word has been replaced by Blacks.

Bantustans   The name given to tribal homelands during the period when Blacks were named Bantu.

Baragwanath Hospital   Africa's biggest hospital, located in Soweto, in the suburbs of Johannesburg.

Barnard, Christiaan   South African doctor who carried out the first successful heart transplant.

Bechuanaland   Name of Botswana while a British protectorate.

Basutoland   Name of Lesotho while a British protectorate.

Biko, Steve   Leader of the Black Consciousness Movement who died in 1977 while in police custody.

Biltong   Strips of sun-dried antelope meat.

Blackburn, Molly   Leading activist in the Black Sash.

Black Consciousness Movement   Organization dedicated to securing the equality of Whites and Blacks with priority of place to Blacks.

Black Sash   Originally a White Womens' movement founded to oppose the removal of the Colored franchise in the 1950s. Members wear black sashes as symbols of protest.

Black spots   Black settlements in White areas of South Africa.

Black township   Residential areas for Blacks in suburbs.

Blacks   Generic term used for the tribes that migrated to Southern Africa from central and western parts of the continent.

Blood River   Name given to the Ncome River in Natal where, in 1838, a small force of Afrikaners turned back a massive Zulu assault. Prior to the encounter, the Afrikaners took an oath, to remember the day as one of deliverance by God if they won. That day, 16 December, is now commemorated annually as the Day of the Vow.

BLS nations   Botswana, Lesotho, Swaziland.

Boer   Dutch for farmer, formerly applied to Afrikaners.

Boer War I   1880, fought over British interference in the affairs of the South African Republic. Won by the Afrikaners.

Boer War II   1899-1902, fought on the pretext of the British defending the political rights of the foreign Rand miners. Won by British and Empire forces against the Afrikaners.

Boesak, Allan   President of the World Alliance of Reformed Churches.

Bophuthatswana   Independent state within South Africa.

Botha, R. F.   South African Minister of Foreign Affairs.

Botha, P. W.   South African State President. With his appointment as President, in 1985, came the end of the parliamentary system which had operated since independence in 1910. The following prime ministers held office during this 75 year period: General L. Botha (1910–19); General J. C. Smuts (1919–24, 1939–48); General J. B. M. Hertzog (1924–39); Dr. D. F. Malan (1948–54); Mr. J. G. Strijdom (1954–58); Dr. H. F. Verwoerd (1958–66); Mr. B. J. Vorster (1966–78); Mr. P. W. Botha (1978–85).

Botswana   Independent nation adjoining South Africa on the West.

Bushmen   Original inhabitants of what is now South Africa.

Buthelezi, Mangosuthu G.   Chief Minister of KwaZulu, a self-governing state, and President of Inkatha.

Cape Coloreds   The mixed-blood people of the Cape.

Cape Flats   Low-lying coastal areas close to Cape Town, often the sites of non-White residential areas.

Cape Malays   Descendants of people brought from the former Dutch East Indies, now Indonesia, in the early days of settlement at Cape Town.

Cape of Good Hope   A promontory extending into the Atlantic near the southernmost tip of the African continent.

Ciskei   Independent state within South Africa.

Color bar   The reservation of certain jobs in commerce and industry for Whites only.

Coloreds   Same as Cape Coloreds.

Commandos   Small groups of soldiers who make surprise attacks. First seen in Boer War II.

Compound   Barracks-like accommodations for migrant laborers who work in the mines around Johannesburg.

Comrades   Young revolutionaries who try to destroy existing patterns of law and order in Black townships.

Concentration camps   Used by the British to house captured women and children during Boer War II. Tens of thousands died in these camps.

Conservative Party (CP)   The official opposition in the South African Parliament, dedicated to maintaining some form of apartheid. A 1982 breakaway group from the National Party.

Council of South African Students (COSAS)   Protest group allied with the United Democratic Front (UDF).

Crossroads   Squatter settlement outside Cape Town.

Customs Union   The free interchange of goods among Bophuthatswana, Botswana, Ciskei, Lesotho, Transkei, Swaziland, and Venda.

Dagga   South African word for marijuana.

Day of the Vow   *See* Blood River.

De Beers Mining Company   Diamond company founded by

Cecil Rhodes.

De Lange, J. P. Professor and Rector of Rand Afrikaans University. Author of 1981 Educational Commission Report.

Dhlomo, Oscar KwaZulu Minister of Education and Culture, and Co-convenor of Indaba.

Dias, Bartolomeu First European to land on what is now South Africa. Sailed as far as the Great Fish River, in 1488, before returning home to Portugal.

Die Stem van Suid-Afrika Afrikaans for The Voice of South Africa. Translated lyrics are as follows:

Ringing out from our blue heavens, from our deep seas breaking round;
Over everlasting mountains where the echoing crags resound;
From our plains where creaking wagons cut their trails into the earth—
Calls the spirit of our Country, of the land that gave us birth.
At thy call we shall not falter, firm and steadfast we shall stand,
At thy will to live or perish, O South Africa, dear land.

Disinvestment Stopping investments in a country as a protest against its policies.

Divestment Withdrawal of money already invested in a country as a protest against its policies.

Dutch Reformed Church (DRC) The single biggest Western Church in South Africa, supported mainly by Afrikaner Whites.

Emergency Decree Drastic security intervention by the State to control outbreaks of violence.

Eminent Persons Group (EPG) Representatives of the Commonwealth, appointed by Heads of Government at Nassau Biennial Meeting, 1985. Asked to visit South Africa to assist in finding a peaceful solution to the country's problems. Report published in 1986.

End Conscription Campaign (ECC) Group seeking abolition of conscription on political grounds.

False Bay Coastal area 25 miles East of Cape Town, site of Khayelitsha (meaning new home) Black Township.

Fanakalo Hybrid language derived from Zulu, Afrikaans

and English. Used in the mines to ensure safety for workers from different language groups.

Forced removals The transfer of non-Whites, mainly Blacks, from areas reserved for Whites to traditional homelands. In many cases, the forced removals created severe hardship, especially among those that had been born in the White areas, and had never known any other homeland.

Fort Hare A community in the independent state of Ciskei, site of South Africa's oldest university for Blacks.

Freedom Charter Policy statement adopted by Asians, Blacks, Coloreds, and Whites, in 1955, as one blueprint for a future South Africa. It says, in part: "That South Africa belongs to all who live in it. . . . That our country will never be prosperous and free until all our people live in brotherhood."

Frontline states Those nations that border South Africa.

Gandhi, Mahatma Indian leader who lived in South Africa between 1893 and 1915, campaigning for Indian rights against the British.

Gazankulu Self-governing state or homeland.

General Affairs Matters of national interest, such as defence and foreign relations, as distinguished from Own Affairs which only concern one population group within the country.

Great Fish River Early border between Xhosa and Dutch and English settlers at the Cape. Now southern boundary of the independent state of Ciskei.

Great Trek The migration of large numbers of Afrikaners into the interior of the country, to establish an independent state beyond the borders of the British Colony.

Griquas A mixed group of people from the Western Cape who settled in the northwestern part of Cape Province.

Group Areas Act The allocation of specific residential areas to different racial or ethnic groups, such as Asians, Blacks, Coloreds, and Whites.

Guguletu Squatter settlement outside Cape Town.

Gumede, Archibald Co-Chair of the United Democratic Front (UDF).

Herstigte Nasionale Party (HNP) The reconstituted National Party, a rebel group which broke away from the

government in 1969, in order to oppose its liberal
tendencies.

Hillbrow Multi-racial residential suburb of Johannesburg.

Homelands Traditional locations for the various Black
tribes. Also known as national states.

Homeland	Tribe
Bophuthatswana	Tswana
Ciskei	Xhosa
Gazankulu	Shangaan and Tsonga
KaNgwane	Swazi
KwaNdebele	Ndebele
KwaZulu	Zulu
Lebowa	North Sotho
Qwaqwa	South Sotho
Transkei	Xhosa
Venda	Venda

Hottentots The original inhabitants of South Africa, who
occupied the land long before Blacks and Whites arrived.

House of Assembly White Chamber in the Tricameral Parliament.

House of Delegates Asians Chamber in the Tricameral
Parliament.

House of Representatives Coloreds Chamber in the Tricameral Parliament.

Huguenots French protestants who fled domestic persecution and settled in South Africa in 1688.

Human Sciences Research Council (HSRC) Organization
which conducts or commissions most of South Africa's
social science research. Publishes an extensive list of reports anually.

Hurley, Denis Roman Catholic Archbishop of Durban.

Identity Card The new universal document identifying all
South Africans, irrespective of ethnic group. For Blacks
it replaced the pass books.

Immorality Act One of the new apartheid laws introduced
after 1948, forbidding sexual intercourse between
Whites and non-Whites. Repealed in 1985.

Impis Zulu soldiers named by King Shaka in the 1820s.

Indaba Zulu word for conference. Usually applied to the
special Natal constitutional conference.

Independent Party (IP) Opposition political party formed in 1987, led by Denis Worrall.

Indians People brought into Natal from India by the British to work in the tea and sugar plantations.

Influx control *See* Pass Books.

Inkatha Zulu for a Black liberation movement founded originally in 1928, then revived by Chief Mangosuthu Buthelezi in 1975. Now headed by Buthelezi, Inkatha is one of the most powerful Black political movements in South Africa.

Inkosi Zulu for chief.

Institute for a Democratic Alternative for South Africa (IDASA) Extra-parliamentary organization directed by Frederik van Zyl Slabbert, designed to obtain greater political cooperation from Blacks.

Institute of Race Relations (IRR) A Johannesburg-based organization which monitors events in the non-White sectors of the country and publishes, among other things, an annual report on the year's events.

Kaffir An Arab word for Blacks. Today it is a derogatory term when used by Whites.

Kairos Document The religious publication prepared by Christian organizations in 1985, outlining a new theology in which God is said to be partisan, taking sides in human conflict situations.

KaNgwane Self-governing state or homeland.

Karoo Hottentot word for arid. A dry plateau land lying north and east of Cape Town, frequently a sheep rearing area.

Khayelitsha *See* False Bay.

Kimberley The place, now a city, where diamonds were discovered in the 1850s.

Knobkerrie Club with knobbed head, traditional Black weapon.

Kopje Afrikaans for small flat-topped hill.

Kraal Afrikaans for a cattle enclosure in a traditional Black village.

Kruger National Park The huge natural wildlife park lying to the northeast of the country. It contains more species than any other park on the continent.

Kruger, Paul Outstanding Afrikaner leader and President of the South African Republic from 1883 to the time of

Boer War II. He took part in the Great Trek of the 1830s.

Krugerrand Name of the official South African one-ounce gold coin.

KwaNdebele Self-governing state or homeland.

KwaZulu Self-governing state or homeland.

Laager The habit among Afrikaners of gathering wagons in a protective circle in the face of danger. The term has come to mean withdrawal into one's own circle when there is pressure or threat from external sources.

Langa Squatter settlement near Cape Town.

Lebowa Self-governing state or homeland.

Lesotho Independent country surrounded by South Africa.

Lobola Bride price paid by a son-in-law to his father-in-law. Traditionally, the currency is cattle.

Luthuli, Albert South African Chief who was awarded the Nobel Peace Prize in 1960 for his non-violent opposition to apartheid.

Mamelodi Black township near Pretoria.

Mandela, Nelson Former leader of the African National Congress, sentenced in 1964 to life in prison for revolutionary activities.

Mandela, Winnie Wife of Nelson Mandela.

Maputo Capital of Mozambique, formerly known as Lourenco Marquez.

Mealies Corn.

Mohair *See* Angora goat.

Mozambique Independent country lying east of South Africa. Since freedom from Portuguese rule in 1974, the nation has been plagued by civil war and is now close to economic collapse.

Namibia Formerly known as Southwest Africa. A German colony until World War I, then a League of Nations protectorate under South Africa. Conferences for independence have included South Africa, U.S., Cuba, USSR, Angola, and the United Nations.

Natal Indian Congress (NIC) Originally set up by Gandhi during his stay in South Africa, as an agency to protect the Indian population. Continues to fight for Indian rights today.

National anthem   *See* Die Stem van Suid-Afrika.

National Democratic Movement (NDM)   Opposition political party formed in 1987, led by Wynand Malan.

National Party (NP)   The party that gained power in 1948. Has produced splinter parties such as CP and HNP.

National Union of Mineworkers (NUM)   Main union representing miners.

Ndebele   The tribal group of the KwaNdebele Homeland.

Necklacing   A barbarous execution method used by Black revolutionaries to silence those within their own community who oppose revolution. The victim is tied, and a gasoline-soaked tire is placed around the neck and set alight.

Nederduitse Gereformeerde Kerk (NGK)   Dutch Reformed Church.

Nguni   The general term used to describe the various tribal groups, such as Zulu and Xhosa, that settled along the eastern seaboard of South Africa.

Nkomati Accord   The 1984 agreement between South Africa and Mozambique under which the former would not give further military support to RENAMO, a revolutionary group within Mozambique, and the latter would stop giving support to the ANC, which had been launching terrorist raids into South Africa from Mozambique.

Nkosi   *See* Inkosi.

North Sotho   The tribal group of the Lebowa Homeland.

Nyanga   Squatter settlement near Cape Town.

Oath of the Covenant   *See* Blood River.

Oppenheimer, Ernest   Former Chairman of Anglo-American Corporation.

Orange Free State   One of four South African provinces.

Own Affairs   Matters that concern only one population group. *See also* General Affairs.

Pan Africanist Congress (PAC)   A group that broke away from the ANC in 1959 because of disagreements on policy. It emphasizes Black consciousness. *See also* Steve Biko.

Pass Books   Documents that had to be carried at all times by Blacks. The books contained details of the person, name of employer and place of work, and whether or not the person had urban residency status. Repealed in 1986.

Population registration A system of classification by which every person is listed as one of: Asian, Black, Colored, White. The classification carries implications for place of residence and opportunities for work. As a result, each year, there are many requests for change of status.

Pietermaritzburg Capital of the Province of Natal.

Pretoria One of the two centres of South Africa's government. The other is Cape Town.

Progressive Federal Party (PFP) Until the election of 1987, this was the main opposition party in Parliament. It is strongly supported by English Whites. *See also* Conservative Party.

Qwaqwa Self-governing state or homeland.

Ramaphosa, Cyril Head of the National Union of Mineworkers.

Rand Both the unit of money in South Africa and the name of the gold-mining district around Johannesburg.

Rand Revolt A serious uprising by White Rand miners shortly after World War I, the result of a decision on the part of management to replace some Whites by lower-paid Black miners.

Republican Term used to describe Afrikaners in Anglo-Boer War II.

Retief, Piet An Afrikaner leader at the time of the Great Trek, who was tricked and killed by a Zulu king while arranging a peace pact.

Rhodes, Cecil Nineteenth-century English administrator and founder of the De Beers diamond mining company. Tried, but failed, to launch a revolution in order to secure British control over the Afrikaner states.

Robben Island Located in Table Bay near Cape Town. Used as a prison during the colonial and independence periods.

Sanctions Economic boycotts of South Africa and other countries, mainly by Western nations. *See also* disinvestment and divestment.

Separate Amenities Act   Regulations whereby Whites and non-Whites had separate facilities, services, and buildings in most of the country. Repealed in 1980.

Shaka   King of the Zulus, who conquered large areas of what is now Northeast South Africa, and for many years successfully resisted all attempts by other tribes to regain their lands.

Shangaan   One of the tribal groups in the Gazankulu Homeland.

Sharpeville   Scene of the tragic killing in 1960 of 69 Black men who were protesting the pass laws.

Sjambok   Afrikaans for a short leather whip.

Smith, Nico   Afrikaner theological professor who resigned his post to become a pastor in the Mamelodi Black Township.

Smuts, Jan   Prime Minister of South Africa prior to the 1948 election; leading Afrikaner general in Boer War II; international statesman who drafted the United Nations document on human rights.

Sotho   *See* North Sotho and South Sotho.

South African Communist Party (SACP)   A banned organization, closely allied with the ANC and UDF. Founded 1921.

South African Congress of Trade Unions (SACTU)   An organization representing several unions with a combined membership of approximately two million.

South African Council of Churches (SACC)   A group of radical churches, mainly English in origin, representing about 25 percent of South Africa's Christians.

South African Defence Force (SADF)   The combined army, navy, and air forces of the nation.

Southern African Development Coordination Conference (SADCC)   A group consisting of the following nine nations, brought together to plan ways and means of removing their economic dependence on South Africa: Angola, Botswana, Lesotho, Malawi, Mozambique, Swaziland, Tanzania, Zambia, and Zimbabwe.

South Sotho   Tribal group of the Qwaqwa Homeland.

Southwest Africa   *See* Namibia.

Southwest African Peoples Organization (SWAPO)   A revolutionary organization attempting to take control of Namibia by force. It is banned in South Africa.

Soweto   Black Township in the suburbs of Johannesburg.

It is the biggest of all South Africa's Black residential areas, with a population of approximately two million.

Squatter camp Territory occupied without title, usually by Blacks who migrate to city areas in search of work.

Suzman, Helen Long-time PFP member and liberal opponent of the present government's policy.

Swart Gevaar Afrikaans word for Black peril.

Swazi Tribal group of the KaNgwane Homeland.

Swaziland Independent state almost surrounded by South Africa.

Tambo, Oliver Former colleague of Nelson Mandela in the ANC before that organization was banned. He now leads the ANC in exile.

TBVC states Transkei, Bophuthatswana, Venda, and Ciskei. These are the homelands that have been given independence by South Africa but are not yet recognized as independent states by the international community.

Tembisa Black Township near Johannesburg.

Terre Blanche, Eugene Head of an extreme right-wing Afrikaner group that is leading the demand for a separate state for Whites.

Terrorism Act A law passed in 1967 by which any suspected terrorist could be detained indefinitely without trial.

Township Term used to describe the Black residential areas in the suburbs.

Transkei Independent state within South Africa.

Transvaal One of the four provinces of South Africa. The name comes from the River Vaal and refers to the territory north of the river.

Trek Afrikaans word for migration, traditionally via ox wagon.

Trekboer Nomadic farmer.

Tricameral Parliament The National Government of 1985, in which Coloreds and Indians, for the first time, share power with Whites.

Treurnicht, Andries Leader of the CP.

Tsonga Tribal group of the Gazankulu Homeland. *See also* Shangaan.

Tswana Tribal group of the Bophuthatswana independent state within South Africa.

Tutu, Desmond Anglican Archbishop of Cape Town, winner of the Nobel Peace Prize in 1984 for his non-violent opposition to apartheid. Since then has become an advocate of sanctions against South Africa.

United Democratic Front (UDF)   A broad alliance of anti-apartheid parties, mostly Black, formed in 1983. Dr. Allan Boesak pioneered the formation of the organization. In recent years the UDF has become a surrogate for the banned ANC.

Uitlander   Afrikaans for foreigner. Historically, it referred to the miners who flocked to the Rand when gold was discovered there.

Ulundi   Capital of KwaZulu.

Umkhonto We Sizwe   Zulu for Spear of the Nation; refers to the military arm of the ANC.

University of South Africa (UNISA)   The large, mainly correspondence university of 100,000 students located in Pretoria.

Vaal   Name of the river which forms the southern border of Transvaal.

Van Zyl Slabbert, Frederik   Former leader of the PFP, and now Head of the Institute for a Democratic Alternative for South Africa (IDASA).

Veld   Open grassland areas with few trees. Highveld and lowveld refer to lands at different elevations.

Venda   Independent state within South Africa. The term also refers to the tribal group who live in the state.

Verwoerd, Henrik   Prime Minister of South Africa from 1958 until his assassination in 1966. He is generally regarded as the architect of the apartheid laws of the 1950s.

Volk   Afrikaans for People or nation.

Voortrekker   Advance trekker. Those who lead a trek.

Vorster, John   Prime Minister from 1966 to 1978.

Walvis Bay   Territory on the Atlantic coast of Namibia which is an integral part of South Africa.

Wiehahn, N. E.   Author of a major 1979 report which recommended much greater freedom for Black trade unions, and the abolition of many restrictive employment practices. His report marked a turning point for the good in the history of labor and industry.

Windhoek   Capital of Namibia.

Witdoeke   Afrikaans for white cloths, which are tied on youths' arms as symbols of their support for law and order.

Witwatersrand   Afrikaans for ridge of white waters. Site of the main Rand gold reef.

Xhosa   The tribal groups of the Ciskei and Transkei homelands.

Zambia   Independent nation north of Botswana.

Zimbabwe   Independent nation north of South Africa.

Zulu   The tribal group of the KwaZulu Homeland and its language.

Zululand   The former name of the self-governing state of KwaZulu.

Notes

1. C. W. De Kiewiet, *A History of South Africa* (Oxford: Clarendon Press, 1941), p. 184.
2. T. R. H. Davenport, "The Beginnings of Urban Segregation in South Africa", *Occasional Paper No. 15* (Grahamstown: Institute of Social and Economic Research, Rhodes University, 1971), p. 1.
3. Andrew Sancton, "Why Should Some Votes Be Worth More Than Others?", Toronto *Globe and Mail*, 02 January, 1987.
4. T. R. H. Davenport, *South Africa: A Modern History*, 3rd ed. (Johannesburg: Macmillan South Africa, 1987), p. 465.
5. Leonard Thompson, *The Political Mythology of Apartheid* (New Haven: Yale University Press, 1985), p. 14.
6. Sydney Maree, Interviewed by Dave Abbott on CKNW Radio, Vancouver, Canada, on 03 June, 1988.
7. Clem Sunter, *The World and South Africa in the 1990s* (Cape Town: Human and Rousseau Publishers, 1987), p. 31.
8. Donella H. Meadows et al., *The Limits to Growth: A Report for the Club of Rome's Project on the Predicament of Mankind* (New York: New American Library, Inc., 1972), p. 66.
9. Ray Chatelin, "No Morality In Tourist Choices", Vancouver *Province*, 23 August, 1987, p. T5, cols. 1–2.
10. Erich Leistner, "Overview of Interaction in Africa", *Africa Institute of South Africa Bulletin*, Vol. 27, No. 9 (1987): 45.
11. Chamber of Mines Report to the U.S. Government, as quoted in Johannesburg *Star*, 11 May, 1988, p. 1.
12. "Africa at a Glance 1988", *Africa Insight*, Vol. 17, No. 4 (July–August 1987): 93.
13. "Doomsday Professor", Johannesburg *Star*, 15 June, 1988, p. 12.
14. Davenport, p. 14.
15. "Africa At a Glance 1988", p. 95.
16. Sandra Burton, "The New Black Middle Class", *Time*, 29 February, 1988, p. 34.
17. Winnie Graham, "Refugees Start New Towns", Johannesburg *Star*, 09 February, 1988, p. 13, col. 1.
18. Terry Glavin, "Politicians, Sechelt Indian Band Celebrate Self-Government", *Vancouver Sun*, 25 June, 1988, p. B1, cols. 1–6.
19. Davenport, p. 47.
20. Piet Retief, as quoted in Leon Louw and Frances Kendall, *South Africa: The Solution* (Bisho: Amagi Publications, 1986), p. 27.

21. Leo Marquard, *The Peoples and Policies of South Africa*, 3rd ed. (London: Oxford University Press, 1962), p. 11.
22. For further information on life at the Cape in the early days of settlement, see Richard Elphick and Hermann Giliomee, *The Shaping of South African Society* (Cape Town: Longmans, 1979).
23. For details on controversies surrounding this particular group of people, see J. S. Marais, *The Cape Colored People* (Johannesburg: University of Witwatersrand Press, 1957).
24. See S. Bhana and B. Pachai, *A Documentary History of Indian South Africans* (Cape Town: David Philip, 1984).
25. See H. C. Marais et al., *The South African Society: Realities and Future Prospects* (Pretoria: Human Sciences Research Council, 1985), pp. 78–81.
26. South African Department of Foreign Affairs, *The New Parliament* (Pretoria: Government Printer, 1984).
27. James Clarke, ed., *Like It Was: The Star 100 Years in Johannesburg* (Johannesburg: Argus Printing & Publishing Company, 1987), p. 1.
28. Paul Kruger, *Memoirs* (New York: Century Company, 1902), p. 391.
29. Ibid., p. 380.
30. Thomas Pakenham, *The Boer War* (London: Wiedenfeld and Nicolson, 1979).
31. L. H. Gann and Peter Duignan, *South Africa: War, Revolution, or Peace?* (Stanford: Hoover Institution Press, 1978), p. 9.
32. Wilhelm Grutter and D. J. van Zyl, *The Story of South Africa* (Cape Town: Human and Rousseau Publishers, 1981), p. 11.
33. South African Bureau for Information, *South Africa 1986: Official Yearbook of the Republic of South Africa* (Pretoria: Government Printer, 1986), p. 201.
34. Hermann Giliomee, "Apartheid: The Myths and the Miseries", Johannesburg *Sunday Times*, 22 May, 1988, p. 19, col. 2.
35. Credo Mutwa, *Let Not My People Die* (Pretoria: United Publishers International, 1986), pp. 79, 183.
36. "Africa at a Glance 1988", p. 33.
37. Simon Barber, "Most Blacks Not In Favour of Sanctions", Pretoria *Business Day*, 16 June, 1988, p. 1.
38. Simon Barber, "Botswana's Plea on U.S. Sanctions Bill", Pretoria *Business Day*, 24 May, 1988, p. 1.
39. Merle Lipton, *Capitalism and Apartheid* (London: Gower/Temple Smith, 1985).
40. Simon Jenkins, "Why Sanctions Are a Failure", *U.S. News and World Report*, 21 September, 1987, p. 40.
41. Simon Barber, "South Africa Has An Answer to Holier Than Thou Sanctions", Pretoria *Sunday Times*, 20 March, 1988, p. 29.
42. Michael Chester, "Informal Sector: Panacea for Unemployment Crisis", Johannesburg *Star*, 08 June, 1988, p. 8, col. 1.
43. Stephen Robinson, "ANC In the Doldrums", Pretoria *Business Day*, 22 April, 1988.
44. Linda Lichter, *The Media Elite: America's New Power Brokers* (New York: Adler and Adler, 1987).
45. Lewis H. Lapham et al., "Can the Press Tell the Truth?", *Harper Magazine*, January 1988, p. 46.
46. George Will, "The Journalist's Role", in *Terrorism and the Media: Abdication of Responsibility*, Proceedings of the Jerusalem Conference on International Terrorism (Jerusalem: The Jonathan Institute, 1979), p. 34.
47. Reed Irvine and Cliff Kincaid, eds., "The Media Target South Africa", in Accuracy in Media, Incorporated, *Aim Report*, October, 1986, p. 1.

48. Robin Friedland, "Fragmentation On the Left", *South Africa Foundation Review*, Vol. 14, No. 6 (June, 1988): 3.
49. *The Kairos Document: Challenge to the Church* (Grand Rapids: William B. Eerdmans Publishing Company, 1985).
50. Richard John Neuhaus, "No Third Way: The Partisan Church in South Africa", *South Africa International*, Vol. 17, No. 1 (July, 1986): 23.
51. G. C. Oosthuizen, "A View of the Black", *Christian Forum*, Vol. 1, No. 4 (Easter, 1988): 12–13.
52. See Walter Wink, *Violence and Nonviolence in South Africa: Jesus' Third Way* (Philadelphia: New Society Publishers, 1987).
53. Alan Paton, "The Beloved Country", *Influence*, February/March, 1988, p. 16.
54. Jurgen Blenk and Klaus von der Ropp, "Republic of South Africa: Is Partition a Solution?", in *South African Journal of African Affairs*, No. 1 (1977), p. 29.
55. R. I. Rotberg and John Barratt, eds., *Conflict and Compromise in South Africa*, (New York: Lexington Books, 1980), p. 120.
56. See Wessel de Kock, *Usuthu! Cry Peace* (Cape Town: Open Hand Press, 1986).
57. Albert P. Blaustein, "What South Africa Needs", *Clarion Call*, Vol. 4 (1985): 97.
58. A. J. A. Peck, "Rhodesia", London *Times*, 19 November, 1965, p. 13, cols. 5–6.
59. Alan Cowell, "Botha Sees South African Churchmen and Falwell", *New York Times*, 20 August, 1985, p. A6, col. 1.
60. Gerald L'Ange, "How South Africa Can Make Capital Out of Ash", Johannesburg *Sunday Star*, 29 November, 1987.
61. "Miners Rate South Africa Above East Germany", Pretoria *Business Day*, 11 July, 1988.
62. Summarized from "Africa at a Glance 1988".

Bibliography

The complexity of South Africa is not easily grasped. This bibliography is therefore provided for the reader who wishes to study particular topics in greater detail.

General

Africa South of the Sahara. London: Europa Publications, 1989.

Africa Institute of South Africa. *Africa Insight*. Pretoria: Africa Institute of South Africa, 1989.

U.S. Bureau of Public Affairs. *Background Notes*. Washington, D.C.: U.S. Government Printing Office, 1989.

Clarke, James. *Our Fragile Land*. Johannesburg: Macmillan of South Africa, 1974.

South African Bureau for Information. *South Africa 1988/1989: Official Yearbook of the Republic of South Africa*. Pretoria: Government Printer, 1989.

Readers Digest. *Atlas of South Africa*. Cape Town: Readers Digest, 1984.

Readers Digest. *Readers Digest Guide to Game Parks*. Cape Town: Readers Digest, 1983.

Saunders, Christopher. *Historical Dictionary of South Africa*. Metuchen, N.J.: Scarecrow, 1983.

South African Institute of Race Relations. *Race Relations Survey*. Johannesburg: South African Institute of Race Relations, 1988.

Biography

Flint, J. *Cecil Rhodes*. Boston: Little, Brown, and Company, 1974.

Gregory, T. *Ernest Oppenheimer and the Economic Development of South Africa*. Cape Town: Oxford University Press, 1962.

Hancock, W. K. *Smuts*. 2 vols. Cambridge: Cambridge University Press, 1968.

Huttenback, R. A. *Gandhi in South Africa*. Ithaca: Cornell University Press, 1971.

Luthuli, A. *Let My People Go*. New York: McGraw Hill, 1962.

Saunders, C., ed. *Black Leaders in South Africa*. London: Heinemann Educational Books, 1979.

Temkin, B. *Gatsha Buthelezi: Zulu Statesman*. Cape Town: Purnell, 1976.

Culture

De Villiers, Marq. *White Tribe Dreaming*. Toronto: Macmillan of Canada, 1987.

Kirby, P. R. *The Musical Instruments of the Native Races of South Africa*. 2nd ed. Johannesburg: University of Witwatersrand Press, 1965.

Kruger, P. *Memoirs*. New York: Century Company, 1902.

Marais, J. S. *The Cape Coloured People*. Johannesburg: University of Witwatersrand Press, 1957.

Michener, James A. *The Covenant*. New York: Random House, 1980.

Paton, Alan. *Cry the Beloved Country*. New York: Charles Scribner's Sons, 1948.

Thomas, Elizabeth Marshall. *The Harmless People*. New York: Alfred A. Knopf, 1958.

Economy

Doxey, G. V. *The Industrial Colour Bar in South Africa*. Cape Town: Oxford University Press, 1961.

Cartwright, A. P. *The Gold Miners*. Cape Town: Purnell and Sons, 1962.

Chilvers, H. A. *The Story of De Beers*. London: Cassell, 1939.

Lipton, M. *Capitalism and Apartheid*. London: Gower/Temple Smith, 1985.

Meadows, Donella H., et al., eds. *The Limits to Growth*. New York: The New American Library, 1972.

Natrass, J. *The South African Economy*. Cape Town: Oxford University Press, 1984.

Stephenson, D. *South Africa's Water Resources*. Johannesburg: University of Witwatersrand, 1983.

Sunter, Clem. *The World and South Africa in the 1990s*. Cape Town: Human and Rousseau, 1987.

History

Bhana, S. and B. Pachai. *A Documentary History of Indian South Africans*. Cape Town: David Philip, 1984.

Brookes, E. H. *A History of Natal*. Pietermaritzburg: Natal University Press, 1965.

Butler, G. *The 1820 Settlers: An Illustrated Commentary*. Cape Town: Human and Rousseau, 1974.

Clarke, James, ed. *Like It Was: The Star One Hundred Years in Johannesburg*. Johannesburg: Argus Printing and Publishing Company, 1986.

Davenport, T. R. H. *South Africa: A Modern History*. 3rd ed. Johannesburg: Macmillan of South Africa, 1987.

De Kiewiet, C. W. *A History of South Africa*. London: Clarendon Press, 1941.

Elphick, Richard. *Kraal and Castle: Khoikhoi and the Founding of White South Africa*. New Haven: Yale University Press, 1977.

Elphick, Richard and Hermann Giliomee, eds. *The Shaping of South African Society*. Cape Town: Longman, 1979.

Grutter, W. *The Story of South Africa*. Cape Town: Human and Rousseau, 1984.

Marquard, L. *The Peoples and Policies of South Africa*. 3rd. ed. London: Oxford University Press, 1962.

Muller, C. F. J., ed. *Five Hundred Years: A History of South Africa*. 3rd ed. Pretoria: Academica, 1981.

Pakenham, Thomas. *The Boer War*. London: Weidenfeld and Nicolson, 1979.

Peires, J. B., ed. *Before and After Shaka: Studies in Nguni History*. Grahamstown: Rhodes University, 1981.

Ross, R. *Adam Kok's Griquas*. Cambridge: Cambridge University Press, 1976.

Walker, C. *The Women's Suffrage Movement in South Africa*. Cape Town: University of Cape Town, 1979.

Walker, E. A. *The Great Trek*. London: A and C Black, 1934.

Politics

Buthelezi, M. G. *White and Black Nationalism: Ethnicity and the Future of the Homelands*. Johannesburg: South African Institute of Race Relations, 1974.

————. *Power Is Ours*. New York: Books in Focus, 1979.

Campbell, William A. B. and Richard K. Melchin. *In Pursuit of Peace and Western Security*. Vancouver: Canadian Conservative Centre, 1988.

De Kock, Wessel. *Usuthu: Cry Peace*. Cape Town: Open Hand Press, 1986.

Gann, L. H. and Peter Duignan. *Why South Africa Will Survive*. London: Croom Helm, 1981.

————. *South Africa: War, Revolution or Peace?* Stanford: Stanford University Press, 1978.

Leach, Graham. *South Africa*. London: Methuen, 1987.

Louw, Leon and Frances Kendall. *South Africa: The Solution*. Bisho: Amagi Publications, 1986.

Mutwa, Credo. *Let Not My Country Die*. Pretoria: United Publishers International, 1986.

Neuhaus, Richard John. *Dispensations: the Future of South Africa as South Africans See It*. Grand Rapids: William B. Eerdmans, 1986.

Phillips, Howard. *Moscow's Challenge to U.S. Vital Interests in Southern Africa*. Vienna, VA: Policy Analysis, Incorporated, 1987.

Quail, George Philip. *Report of the Ciskei Commission*. Pretoria: Conference Associates, 1980.

Sater, H. *The South African Flag Controversy*. Cape Town: Oxford University Press, 1980.

Smock, G. E. *Gold in the Furnace*. Shreveport: Huntington House, 1987.

Tennyson, B. D. *Canadian Relations with South Africa*. Washington, D.C.: University Press of America, Incorporated, 1982.

Thomashausen, A. E. A. M. *The Dismantling of Apartheid*. Cape Town: Printpak Books, 1987.

Thompson, Leonard. *The Political Mythology of Apartheid*. New Haven: Yale University Press, 1985.

Van Vuuren, D. J., ed. *South African Election*. Durban: Owen Burgess, 1987.

Religion

De Gruchy, J. *The Church Struggle in South Africa*. Grand Rapids: William B. Eerdmans Publishing Company, 1979.

Hexham, Irving. *The Irony of Apartheid: the Struggle For National Independence of Afrikaner Calvinism Against British Imperialism.* New York: Edwin Mellen, 1981.

Human Sciences Research Council. *Religion, Intergroup Relations and Social Change in South Africa.* Pretoria: Human Sciences Research Council, 1985.

The Kairos Document: Challenge To the Church. Grand Rapids: William B. Eerdmans, 1985.

Wink, Walter. *Violence and Nonviolence in South Africa: Jesus' Third Way.* Philadelphia: New Society, 1987.

Society

Davenport, T. R. H. *The Beginnings of Urban Segregation in South Africa.* Grahamstown: Rhodes University Institute of Social and Economic Research, 1971.

Baggaley, J., et al., eds. *Evaluation of Educational Television.* Johannesburg: South African Broadcasting Corporation, 1987.

Godsell, R. M. *Growth, Equity and Participation.* Pretoria: Human Sciences Research Council, 1986.

Human Sciences Research Council. *The South African Society: Realities and Future Prospects.* Pretoria: Human Sciences Research Council, 1985.

Levitas, B. *South Africa: Tribal Life Today.* Cape Town: College Press, 1984.

Lichter, L. *The Media Elite: America's New Power Brokers.* New York: Adler and Adler, 1987.

Malherbe, E. G. *Education in South Africa.* 2 vols. Cape Town: Juta, 1977.

Shepherd, R. H. W. *Lovedale, South Africa: The Story of a Century, 1841–1941.* Lovedale: Lovedale Press, n.d.

Van Vuuren, D. J., et. al., eds. *Change in South Africa.* Durban: Butterworths, 1983.

————. *South Africa: A Plural Society in Transition.* Durban: Butterworths, 1985.

Index

Johannesburg, 31, 53, 92, 110,
  156, 170, 186, 188, 190, 194,
  195; informal sector, 88; rail
  connections, 181, 182; Regional
  Services Council, 155;
  urbanization, 29, 67, 91; water
  needs, 90. *See also*
  Pretoria/Witwatersrand/
  Vereeniging (PWV) Complex
Johannesburg *Financial Mail*, 126
Johannesburg *Star*, vii, 52, 120
John Paul II, 128
Judiciary, 153

Kairos Document, 129, 130
Kalahari Desert, 23, 31
KaNgwane, 33. *See also* Homelands
Karoo, 87, 88
Kei River, 32
Khayelitsha, 70, 72
Khoikhoi, 181
Khoisan, 23, 25
Kimberley, 51, 56, 139, 181
Koppel, Ted, 118, 119
Kruger, S. J. P., 36, 50, 53, 54, 55,
  182
Kruger National Park, 17, 31, 33
Krugerrands, 79, 92
Krugersdorp, 156
Ku Klux Klan, 163
KwaNdebele, 33. *See also*
  Homelands
KwaZulu, vii, ix, 34, 128, 138, 142,
  143, 144. *See also* Homelands
KwaZulu Natal Indaba, 143, 145,
  146; Joint Executive, 9, 147;
  State President, 146

Labor Party, 94
Land distribution, 27, 46, 93, 153
Langa, 70
Langlaagte, 52
Latin America, 79, 162
Lebanon, 19
Lebowa, 34. *See also* Homelands
Legislative Powers, 49
Leipzig, 171
Lesotho, 34, 40, 144, 153, 154, 168,
  169, 170, 175, 181;
  independence, 173; South
  African immigration from, 69
Lesotho Highlands Water Project,
  90, 171
Lilongwe, 175
Limpopo River, 24, 42

Lippmann, Walter, 67
Lipton, Merle, 78
Livingstone, David, 42
London, 61, 149
London *Times*, 162
Lourenco Marquez, 191
Luanda, 174
Lusaka, 178
Lusaka Manifesto, 172

Madagascar, 38
Magersfontein Ridge, 56
Mafeking, 56
Malan, D. F., 43, 185
Malan, Wynand, 126, 192
Malawi, 40, 168, 169, 170, 175, 182
Malays, 45, 46
Mandela, Nelson, 149, 165.
Mao Tse-Tung, 62
Maple Leaf (gold coin), 79
Maputo, 52, 171, 176
Maree, Sydney, 9
Maseru, 175
Mauritania, 28
Mbabane, 178
McLuhan, Marshall, 13
Mecca, 46, 67
Media, 1, 2, 7, 8, 13, 99, 100, 105,
  115-121; confidence in, 118
Medical University of South Africa,
  71
Mediterranean Sea, 77
Metal products, 16, 80, 85, 91, 92,
  170, 176, 178
Methodist Church, 132
Mexico, 13
Milner, Alfred, 54, 60, 61, 63
Mineral Resources, 16, 17, 31, 33,
  34, 80, 83, 91, 92, 93, 170, 177
Mining 15, 17, 92, 98, 136, 173,
  182; effects of Black
  enfranchisement on, 126;
  immigration due to, 68, 94, 171;
  safety, 74, 126; union, 192, 193;
  urbanization effect, 90; violence
  with Mozambiquans, 172
Minister of Constitutional
  Development and Planning, 146-
  147
Minister of Education, 111
Ministers' Councils, 48, 147, 161
Mokoena, Isaac, 131. *See also*
  Religion
Moscow, 3, 97, 100, 119